# MARRIAGE
# IS FOR
# LOVE

# MARRIAGE IS FOR LOVE

RICHARD L. STRAUSS

Tyndale House Publishers, Wheaton, Illinois

Coverdale House Publishers Ltd., London, England

Library of Congress Catalog Card Number 73-81007; ISBN 8423-4180-3 cloth; 8423-4181-1 paper; Copyright © 1973 Tyndale House Publishers, Wheaton, Illinois; First printing, June 1973; Printed in the United States of America

TO MARY
FAITHFUL HELPMEET
EVER GROWING IN CHRISTLIKE LOVE

# CONTENTS

# CHAPTER ONE

# CAN TWO WALK TOGETHER?

Sue had just gotten back from her honeymoon, yet here she was, pouring out her tragic tale. Marriage just wasn't what she had expected. The glow of those courtship days was already waning. Bob's attentive devotion was turning to unreasonable demands and caustic criticism, and she could feel the bitterness rising inside her. I wasn't surprised to hear that another marriage was in trouble, but . . . so soon?

While the timing of Bob and Sue's problem may have been exceptional, the reality of it is all too typical. Let's face it — the institution of marriage has come upon hard times. Psychiatrists, psychologists, and sociologists are telling us that the foundations for stable homes have already been eroded, and that the whole institution is in danger of collapse. Statistics seem to support their claim. In 1900 about one in twelve marriages ended in divorce. By 1922 the number had risen to one in eight. Right now about one in three marriages ends in divorce! Since most divorces produce emotional scars that adversely affect the marriages of the following generations, the prospect is even more bleak for the future.

There's more. Census reports indicate that a frightening number of husbands and wives live separated from each other. Add to this the millions of couples who live under the same roof but are separated in spirit, and the outlook is even dimmer. Sometimes these homes are openly acknowledged battlegrounds, and sometimes there is a mutually tolerated truce — he goes his way and she goes hers, and never the twain shall meet! They may remain married for the sake of the children or for their reputations, but instead of enjoying heavenly bliss they endure a virtual hell on earth.

After interviewing two thousand married couples, one prominent marriage counselor reported that 70 percent of the women and 60 percent of the men would not marry the same partner if they had it to do over! Many reported that they wouldn't marry at all! As a pastor in whom people confide, I can attest that Christian homes are not exempt from this kind of marital unhappiness. We hear of marital unfaithfulness among Christians, of resentment and bitterness between Christian marriage partners, of loud outbursts of temper, of long periods of silence, of cutting criticism and declining affection. All of these are symptoms of sick and unhappy homes. Such people are a poor advertisement of the peace, purpose, and power which Jesus Christ offers. For Christ's sake, as well as for our own well-being, we need to give serious attention to making our marriages work.

What is causing the breakdown of our homes? Sociologists have suggested several reasons for it:

1) Mobility. One out of three families in which the husband is under thirty-five moves each year. This tends to breed insecurity and instability.

2) The depersonalization of human beings in our computerized society. The resultant loneliness, aimlessness, frustration, despair, and self-pity are certainly not conducive to successful marriages.

3) The sexual revolution. Premarital and extramarital affairs are among the most deadly and destructive forces attacking marriage today.

4) Affluence. Our materialistic culture practically eliminates the meaningful interpersonal relationships necessary for a happy home.

5) Growing permissiveness in training children. We are producing an undisciplined generation of young people who are poorly equipped to establish successful homes.

6) Radio and TV. Their shallow portrayals of love and their addictive tyranny of time make an effective home life most difficult.

This multi-faceted assault on the home is really not surprising. The Bible teaches that marriage and the family are divine institutions. In fact, they were the first institutions established by God. He views them as essential elements in accomplishing his purposes for the human race. For this reason we can expect Satan to attack them. However, his attacks need not be successful. The God who ordained marriage in the first place can certainly make it work today!

Yours *can* be a happy Christian home if you will learn and practice the basic biblical principles of marriage. I believe that any normally intelligent husband and wife can enjoy a happy marriage and a successful home life if they learn what the Bible teaches and obey it. Everything necessary to establish such a relationship is found in the Scriptures. These biblical principles will be of greatest value only if both husband and wife study them and claim God's power to obey them. Even if only one partner obeys, however, there will still be a tremendous improvement in the marriage, and the obedience will have been well worth the effort! If both partners respond, their home can become a little taste of heaven.

On Christmas day, six months before I married, my fiancée gave me a new Bible in which she inscribed a little note and an obscure reference from the Old Testament: "Can two walk together, except they be agreed?"[1] This was originally spoken by God to the nation Israel, but it also contains a practical message for every couple who would like to enjoy a successful marriage today. Each must agree to do his or her part before the Lord. You might be walking together a long time before the return of Jesus Christ! Join hands with your partner and say, "With Christ's help I want to make this marriage and this home the kind that will bring glory to God."

My heart goes out to Christians married to unbelievers. They can never be fully agreed, since one partner has Christ living within

---

[1] Amos 3:3, King James Version.

and the other does not. Sometimes Christians arrive at this mixed situation because they trusted Christ after they married. If they will faithfully obey God's marriage instructions, they may well be able to lead their mates to the Savior.

But a word of warning is in order for Christians contemplating marriage. It is utterly foolish for a believer to knowingly and willfully marry an unbeliever. The Word of God clearly forbids it, and the disobedient Christian cannot expect God's blessing on his or her marriage. The Apostle Paul assures widows that they may remarry, but "only in the Lord."[2] Paul also gives this specific command, which certainly includes the marriage relationship: "Be ye not unequally yoked together with unbelievers: for what fellowship hath righteousness with unrighteousness? and what communion hath light with darkness? And what concord hath Christ with Belial? or what part hath he that believeth with an infidel?"[3] Paul is drawing upon the Old Testament law which prohibited Jews from yoking together two different kinds of animals such as an ox and a donkey.[4] Because the animals were incompatible, the mixed yoke was unfair to both of them. For this same reason we are to avoid intimate unions with unbelievers.

Did you notice the words employed in this passage to describe the incompatibility of such a union?

1) There can be no *fellowship*. Fellowship means sharing or participation. A forgiven person and an unforgiven person have little in common; they cannot share their lives in happy interrelationships.

2) There can be no *communion*. This word refers to mutual association, close relationship, or intimate interaction. It is usually translated "fellowship," like the first word, but it is more personal, involving the sharing of ourselves personally. What intimate association can light have with darkness? They cannot exist in the same

[2] 1 Corinthians 7:39, KJV.    [3] 2 Corinthians 6:14, 15, KJV.    [4] Deuteronomy 22:10.

place at the same time; they are incompatible. And so are a believer and an unbeliever, no matter what their feelings may have been before marriage! The believer is "full of light" while the unbeliever is "full of darkness."[5] They simply cannot harmonize!

3) There can be no *concord*. From this word, meaning literally, "to blend voices together," we get our English word "symphony." A partner who belongs to Christ and one who does not cannot make sweet music together. They may think they will be able to, but God says they will produce dissonance and discord!

4) There can be no *part*. This refers to a share or portion which contracting parties hold in agreement. The potential for full agreement and complete harmony simply does not exist between believers and unbelievers, and it is therefore unfair to each party to yoke them together.

If you are contemplating marriage to an unbeliever, pause and think with me. You are really being unfair to the person you intend to marry. Your intended partner thinks your heart belongs exclusively to him (or her), but it does not. You share your love with Christ! In a Christian marriage, this sharing draws the husband and wife closer to each other, but *not in a mixed marriage!* Your love for Christ and your love for your unsaved mate will often conflict, resulting in turmoil and strife. You shouldn't even consider subjecting the one you claim to love to that kind of unpleasantness. Marital adjustments are difficult enough without amplifying them by an obstacle of this magnitude.

Neither are you being fair to yourself. Mixed marriages are forbidden all the way through the Bible, in the Old Testament as well as in the New Testament.[6] God says that the unbeliever may turn the believer's heart away from the Lord. If that happens, God will have to bring you back to the happiness and satisfaction of fellowship with himself. You may undergo one trial after another until you

---

[5]Ephesians 5:8, *The Living Bible*. All quotations from TLB are by permission of Tyndale House Publishers.    [6]e.g. Deuteronomy 7:3, 4.

yield yourself totally to the Lord — and then your unsaved mate will probably be unhappy about it!

Finally, you are being unfair to God. He sent his Son to Calvary's cross to die for your sins so that he could have you for himself.[7] To give yourself instead to someone who does not belong to Christ is not fair to the God who saved you. God established Christian marriage as a beautiful picture of the relationship that exists between Christ and his church. The better your marriage pictures that divine union, the better will be your Christian witness to a lost world. Since marriage with an unbeliever caricatures this divine picture, you will mar your testimony by entering this kind of mixed relationship. This is grossly unfair to God.

Maybe you're saying, "But I'll win my mate to Christ after the wedding." God never intended marriage to be a mission field! Occasionally an unsaved partner is won to Christ, but the overwhelming odds are against you. The tension produced by your willful disobedience to God's command will not be conducive to effective evangelism. Why not do it God's way? Ask him to lead you to the life partner of *his* choice. You'll never be sorry!

If these words of advice are too late, and you have already made the mistake of marrying an unbeliever, do not despair. God is a forgiving Father. Acknowledge your disobedience to him, then read on. He will show you how you can improve your marital relationship, and you may even become one of that small number who have led their spouses to the Savior.

One thing should have become abundantly clear as you read through this chapter. The Lord Jesus Christ is the key to a successful marriage. The chances of making your marriage work apart from him are nil. If you are not certain about your spiritual condition, you may be the partner who is responsible for the tension

[7]Titus 2:14.

and turmoil of an unequal alliance. Now is the time to remedy that situation.

At issue is more than simply an intellectual knowledge of Christianity. At issue is *a personal relationship with the Lord Jesus Christ himself.* Here is how we enter that relationship. We first acknowledge our sinfulness and our total inability to earn the favor of an infinitely holy God.[8] We acknowledge that Christ died in our place, thereby paying the penalty for our sins.[9] We place our total personal trust in Christ as our sacrifice for sin, thereby receiving him as our Savior. He thereupon bestows on us his gracious gift of eternal salvation.[10] If you have never made this decision, why not do it now? Give your marriage a chance to succeed! Receive Christ as your personal Savior from sin!

[8]Romans 3:23; Isaiah 64:6.    [9]Romans 5:8; 1 Peter 2:24.    [10]Romans 6:23; Acts 16:31; John 1:12; 1 John 5:11-13.

# CHAPTER TWO

# THEY SHALL BE ONE

Marriage is a divine institution established by God for man's good. Yet we find it to be a most puzzling phenomenon! On one hand are great numbers of people who cannot wait to get into it, while on the other hand are multitudes of people trying desperately to get out of it! What is this all about? The only real way to find out is to start at the beginning, with the story of creation in the first chapter of Genesis.

As we read along in the narrative we learn that everything God made was good. Seven times over God saw that what he had made was good.[1] Then suddenly we read, "And the Lord God said, it is *not* good. . . ." What was not good? "It is not good that man should be alone!"[2] Adam wasn't really alone, was he? He had all those animals, some of which are reputed to be man's best friends! Yet all those friendly animals were merely living creatures, while Adam was a living soul.[3] He could have no soul-satisfying communion with them. God knew that Adam was alone and that he needed a companion.[4]

Loneliness is an awful thing; it is emptiness, incompleteness, lack of communion, lack of personal companionship. Loneliness is the lack of opportunity to share yourself with someone who understands — someone with whom you can enjoy a mutual commitment and trust. That was Adam's condition when God first made him. Though Adam needed God first and foremost, God said that he also needed a companion.

Does this mean that a man without a wife is less than complete? Yes! — unless he has the divinely bestowed gift of celibacy! The Bible teaches that celibacy is a special gift from God which is sometimes bestowed on a man or woman when the single status would

[1]Genesis 1:4, 10, 12, 18, 21, 25, 31.    [2]Genesis 2:18, KJV.    [3]Genesis 2:7.
[4]Genesis 2:18, 20.

permit him or her to be more effective in the service of Jesus Christ.[5]

Generally speaking, however, it is not good for a man to be alone. "I will make him a helpmeet" was God's proclamation. The word *helpmeet* is derived from two Hebrew words meaning "a help" and "agreeing to him." Woman was created to be a helper suitable for man, compatible with him spiritually, mentally, emotionally, and physically. She is his complement, providing what he lacks and fulfilling his potential.

So God administered the first anesthetic and performed the first surgery. He took a rib out of the man and from it made a woman.[6] While he created man out of the constituents of soil, he made woman out of man. She is part of him. In fact, she *has* part of him, and man is incomplete until he gets that part back in the person of a wife. Notice which part God used — the rib. Saint Augustine wrote, "If God had meant woman to rule over man he would have taken her out of Adam's head. Had he designed her to be his slave, he would have taken her out of his feet. But God took woman out of man's side, for he made her to be a helpmeet and an equal to him." A man's wife is his partner — not his property!

It may seem rather demeaning to a woman that she was made to be a man's helper, but this role actually glorifies her, since man is incomplete without her! Each party needs the other. It was a happy day for both the man and the woman when God gave the first bride away. The man immediately recognized that his wife was part of him, and so he gave her the feminine form of his own name, woman.[7]

The next words in the narrative were spoken by God himself, as Christ attested many years later. "Therefore shall a man leave his father and his mother, and shall cleave unto his wife; and they shall be one flesh."[8] From that moment on, the divine institution of marriage was established. Did you notice the words *leave father and*

[5]Matthew 19:11, 12; 1 Corinthians 7:7, 8, 25, 26.   [6]Genesis 2:21, 22.
[7]Genesis 2:23.   [8]Genesis 2:24, KJV; cf. Matthew 19:4, 5.

*mother?* It is interesting that God should specify this at the very beginning of the human race. In-laws, which continue to be one of the great sources of marital discord, would cause very few problems indeed if husbands and wives would leave their fathers and mothers, just as the Lord commanded, and instead fulfill their primary responsibility to their partners in marriage.

The words *cleave unto* reveal the nature of the marriage bond as God intended it to be. The idea seems to be that a man is to glue himself to his wife. When two inanimate objects are glued together they become a single object. When two people are glued together they likewise become one. God said, *"And they shall be one flesh."* While the words *one flesh* refer basically to the sexual union, there is much more involved than this. When God brings a man and a woman together, he unites them in a unique and profound biological-spiritual bond that reaches to the very depths of their souls.

Marriage should be infinitely more than a piece of paper signed by a minister and infinitely more than two people living under the same roof or sharing the same bed. It should be such a perfect and complete welding together of two personalities that they become one entity. It should be the total commitment of two wills to each other, the blending of two minds into a single mind, the mutual expression of two sets of God-given emotions. Its goal is perfect oneness, total intimacy, and the unhindered sharing of each partner's innermost thoughts, feelings, and very being.

This is a far cry from the common notion that marriage simply provides legalized sex for two people who are physically attracted to each other. God created sex, but he intended it to be a beautiful expression of the oneness of heart and soul that already exists. If that oneness does not exist, the physical act is meaningless, self-centered, and exploitative.

What we learn from the Bible, then, is that marriage was given by God as a sacred union in which one man and one woman are brought together to complement and fulfill each other. An understanding of this basic fact will protect a couple from many marital problems. Husbands and wives who realize that God has joined them into a single entity will not foolishly try to hurt each other, for they know they would only be hurting themselves. Each partner remembers to express genuine love and understanding to the other, for one's mate is really part of one's own self.

There is another application of this passage, an application which Christ himself made. When God brings a man and a woman together in his sovereign will and welds them into one, he intends for that relationship to be permanent. "No man may divorce what God has joined together."[9] Many people seem to have the idea that if a marriage doesn't work they can always terminate it. They wonder why two people would want to invest the effort and sacrifice necessary for a successful marriage when it would be so much easier simply to call it quits. That erroneous concept can be a most serious deterrent to the success of a marriage.

When the Pharisees questioned Christ about the divorce provisions of the Mosaic Law, he told them why they were given: "Moses did that in recognition of your hard and evil hearts." But he quickly added, "But it was not what God had originally intended!"[10] When God glues two people together he intends for them to stick! If we could see marriage in the light of the oneness God desires it to be, divorce would be like amputating an arm or a leg. You do not consider cutting off your arm when you get a splinter in your finger; you try to get the splinter out. Nor should you consider cutting off your husband or your wife because you have not yet been able to adjust to some unpleasant characteristic in him or her. It is our prayer that these lessons will help you get the irritating splinters out of your marriage.

[9]Matthew 19:6b, TLB.    [10]Matthew 19:8, TLB.

There is a difference of opinion among Bible scholars as to whether Christ permitted divorce and remarriage at all. He said that divorce and remarriage constituted adultery except in the case of fornication.[11] Some interpret the words "except it be for fornication" as valid grounds for divorce and remarriage. Others assert that the exception clause does not apply to the marriage relationship as we know it today, and that there are actually no biblical grounds at all for divorce and remarriage. But whichever way they interpret the exception clause, almost all scholars agree on Christ's primary point in this discourse — that God wants marriage to be permanent. He expects us to look for ways to heal our marriages rather than for excuses to dissolve them.

There is also a difference of opinion about the Apostle Paul's teaching on divorce and remarriage. He said, "But if the husband or wife who isn't a Christian is eager to leave, it is permitted."[12] Some think this frees a believer to remarry if the unbelieving mate obtains a divorce. Others say it does not. But whichever way they interpret these words, almost all Bible students agree that Paul's general rule for marriage was established at the outset of his discussion — "A wife must not leave her husband . . . and the husband must not divorce his wife."[13]

This is a controversial subject, and it will never enjoy complete unanimity of interpretation this side of heaven. For this reason we should be careful to maintain an attitude of graciousness and Christlike love toward the casualties of a broken home. But the basic intent of the biblical teaching is undeniable; we must not overlook it. Divorce is not intended as an easy escape for couples who cannot solve their marital problems. The road to happiness in marriage does not consist of unloading one's mate and finding a new one, but rather of *becoming a new mate* by God's grace and power.

"The grass is always greener on the other side of the fence"

---

[11]Matthew 19:9.    [12]1 Corinthians 7:15, TLB.    [13]1 Corinthians 7:10, 11, TLB.

applies as much to marriage as it does to many other areas of life. Some who have managed to climb over the fence have found that the same unpleasant personality traits which produced conflict and tension in their first marriage are now causing problems in their second! They may have gotten new spouses, but they themselves are the same selfish, immature individuals they always were.

I will never forget the desperation in Duane's voice as he sat across from my desk and described the unbelievable chaos of his second marriage. Though he professed to be a Christian, he had five years earlier walked out on Nan to marry another woman, using every rationalization he could muster to justify his actions. What a terrible mistake it had been! Now his second marriage was in shambles too, and he longed for the modest degree of happiness he had once shared with his first wife. He longed to remarry her.

But Duane needed to experience several basic changes in his attitude before he could enjoy success in any marriage relationship. Because many of us are like Duane, we need to consider these important changes as they are discussed in the next several chapters.

# CHAPTER THREE

# IN STEP WITH THE SPIRIT

I am convinced that most Christian marital discord is rooted in personal spiritual problems. In other words, the underlying reason for most of the disharmony we observe in Christian marriages today is *spiritual disorder in one or more of the persons involved.*

We have learned that marriage is a divine institution — that God made man and woman to complete and fulfill each other. When a redeemed man and a redeemed woman join themselves to each other in mutual love and trust, God joins them into a single entity. He expects them to be one in purpose, in motivation, in interests, in understanding, and in sympathies. What we often see in practice, however, is anything but oneness. Many Christian homes are characterized by disunity, arguing, screaming, and pouting. Everyone in the family seems to be pulling in opposite directions, and the result is chaos. Harmony will never be achieved until everyone learns to pull *in the same direction!* This is true spiritual adjustment.

It's always easier to learn about those aspects of marriage which apply to the *other* partner. Women frequently enjoy discussing the husband's responsibility to love his wife. Husbands often enjoy emphasizing the woman's role of submission. But neither the husband nor the wife can fulfill his or her role in marriage without the supernatural power of the indwelling Holy Spirit. And we cannot have the Holy Spirit unless we have received Jesus Christ as our personal Savior from sin!

Most of us want to be the husbands or wives that we ought to be. But we simply cannot become such in our own strength. The Apostle Paul declared, "I know I am rotten through and through so far as my old sinful nature is concerned."[1] We face tremendous physical, emotional, and mental adjustments in marriage. The relationship is

[1]Romans 7:18, TLB.

burdened with divergent backgrounds, differences of opinion, and daily misunderstandings. Two egos, each selfish and sinful, seek individual satisfaction and well-being. The odds against marital bliss seem almost insurmountable! However, the odds can be overcome by supernatural help. The indwelling Holy Spirit longs to help us. Let's find out how to receive his power!

The Apostle Paul divides the human race into three major categories. The first category he labels the "natural" or "soulish" man.[2] His human spirit has never been made alive toward God. He is spiritually dead;[3] he needs to be saved.[4] His life is dominated by his "flesh" — his sinful nature. It is this nature which accounts for all of his weaknesses, such as the anger and jealousy which produce so much turmoil in marriage.

The second group Paul labels the "spiritual" man.[5] This kind of person has received Jesus Christ as his Savior and has allowed the indwelling Holy Spirit to fill his life. He is a mature, stable, and spiritually strong person.

The third category is the "carnal" or "fleshly" man.[6] This person is a Christian, but his sin nature ("the flesh") seems to control him much of the time, producing the same selfishness, anger, worry, jealousy, bitterness, and resentment that he had before he met the Lord.

Now imagine two flesh-dominated lives trying to become perfectly united in daily living! The attempt is futile; each person merely succeeds in partially satisfying his own selfish desires. It matters little whether both parties are unsaved, or both are carnal Christians, or one is unsaved and the other is saved but carnal. The result is much the same in every case.

Even if one of the two parties is controlled by the Holy Spirit, perfect oneness is still impossible to attain. This marriage will be happier than in the previous case, because at least one partner is

---

[2] 1 Corinthians 2:14.  [3] Ephesians 2:1.  [4] Acts 16:31.  [5] 1 Corinthians 2:15.
[6] 1 Corinthians 3:1.

manifesting the love of Christ. But the potential for *perfect* harmony is absent. No sinful ego has the same aspiration, the same motivation, or the same power as the Spirit-dominated life. The two partners will continue to cherish two diametrically opposed sets of goals and values.

Perfect unity comes only when the Holy Spirit fully controls *both lives and draws them together into unity and harmony.* Because the Holy Spirit is a real Person, he can establish goals, direct motives develop attitudes, and assist actions. Because he is God, he exercises all the power required to achieve his goals. Because he is a Spirit, he indwells two partners simultaneously and unites them in heart. There is no way for a husband and wife to enjoy perfect oneness apart from the Spirit-controlled life.

Look at it another way. The Apostle Paul wrote, "If we live in the Spirit, let us also walk in the Spirit."[7] The word "walk" in this verse is a military term used in secular Greek literature to describe rows of soldiers marching in step. If every soldier watches his commanding officer and keeps in step with him, then he will also be in step with every other soldier. Similarly, if a husband and wife both stay in step with the Holy Spirit they will also be in step with each other. It cannot be otherwise.

Look at it still another way. A geometrical axiom states that all objects close to a given object are also close to each other. Apply that axiom to marriage, and you discover that as two people draw close to the Lord they also become close to each other! The believer is a three-part being composed of spirit, soul, and body. The spirit communes with God. The soul is the personality — intellect, emotions, and will. The body possesses five senses through which it experiences various sensations. *Oneness in marriage requires unity in spirit, soul, and body.* Many Christian couples have worked hard at establishing oneness of body through sex and oneness of

---

[7]Galatians 5:25, KJV.

soul through personality interaction, but have tragically neglected the most important unity of all — that of their spirits! They seldom pray together. They rarely share the Word of God with each other. They hardly ever discuss mutual spiritual matters. The Lord is simply not a real part of their relationship with each other. As a result the two partners suffer alienation from each other at the highest plane of their human makeup. This disunity of spirit then disrupts the harmony of soul and body as well. It is God's will that we yield our spirits totally to him. Then he will grant harmony of body and soul as well.

It is significant that the major biblical instruction about the Spirit-filled life is found in a context dealing with marriage.[8] It begins, "And be not drunk with wine, in which is excess, but be filled with the Spirit." Just as a person who is filled with wine is controlled by that wine, so a Christian who is filled with the Spirit is controlled by the Spirit. The verses that follow enumerate four characteristics of Spirit-filled Christians.

1) Speaking to yourselves in psalms, hymns, and spiritual songs.[9]
2) Singing and making melody in your heart to the Lord.[10]
3) Giving thanks always for all things.[11]
4) Submitting yourselves one to another in the fear of God.[12]

This last characteristic describes an attitude of gracious humility and mutual respect. With this mutual submission Paul begins the most extensive discussion of the husband-wife relationship to be found anywhere in the New Testament. None of us can fulfill our divinely revealed responsibilities until we are controlled and empowered by the Holy Spirit of God. There is really no point in reading on and learning what God the Holy Spirit wants to do in our lives unless we are willing to let *him* provide the necessary power. When we do allow him to express his life through us we will not only become worshipful, thankful, and humble, but the ninefold

---

[8]Ephesians 5:18-33.   [9]Ephesians 5:19a, KJV.   [10]Ephesians 5:19b, KJV.
[11]Ephesians 5:20, KJV.   [12]Ephesians 5:21, KJV.

fruit of the Spirit will be evidenced in our lives: love, joy, peace, longsuffering, gentleness, goodness, faith, meekness, and self-control.[13] Dissension is impossible when these are radiating from our lives!

If the filling of the Spirit is the primary issue in a Christian marriage, we need to know how the Holy Spirit can fill us. Here are some suggestions.

1) Examine your life in the light of God's Word.[14] When problems occur in our marriages, the first thing we usually do is to pick at the faults in our mates. As Christ put it, we try to get the splinters out of their eyes while ignoring the logs in our own. Jesus said, "Hypocrite! First get rid of the board. Then you can see to help your brother."[15] If we are honest we will find that we are far from guiltless. We may discover such sins as anger, resentment, bitterness, unkindness, pride, unforgiveness, coldness, selfishness, jealousy, worry, covetousness, and lust. Any one of these can produce untold discord in the home! When we react angrily to the display of these sins in our mates, we ourselves are sinning and are compounding the problem still further.

2) Confess your sins to God.[16] Having discovered our sins, we must promptly acknowledge them by name to God and confess our full responsibility for their appearance. We cannot excuse our outbursts by pointing to our mates' provocations. We are volitional creatures; we can choose to trust God for victory over these outbursts if we wish to. First John 1:9 assures us that God will freely forgive us the moment we confess our sins to him. When we honestly admit to ourselves and to God that our sin is really sin, many of our marital problems start getting solved immediately!

3) Yield every area of your life to God.[17] God wants us to make ourselves wholly available to him, to give ourselves to him with no strings attached. Some people seem to be afraid to commit

---

[13]Galatians 5:22, 23, KJV.    [14]1 Corinthians 11:28, 31.    [15]Matthew 7:5, TLB.    [16]1 John 1:9.    [17]Romans 12:1.

their lives to God; they fear he might make some unreasonable demand or try to harm them in some way. We sometimes find it so hard to believe that God's way is perfect — that he never makes mistakes.[18] We desperately need to commit our lives totally to Christ. Only then can we become filled and controlled by the Holy Spirit. If we refuse to relinquish our wills to him, it will shrivel our entire personality, making us unbearable to live with and destroying the potential for perfect marital harmony. Let's get our marriages on the right footing; let's do it God's way!

Countless Christians have already discovered that their seemingly hopeless marriages were transformed into beautiful harmony when they yielded their lives unreservedly to Christ. Some have discovered this secret only after long battles and bitter heartaches. Why not obey God's Word right now and avoid all the heartaches? The improvement in your marriage can begin today!

4) The Spirit-filled Christian finds such joy and satisfaction in his yielded relationship with the Spirit of God that he wants to maintain it continually. He does so by constantly acknowledging the Holy Spirit's indwelling power. He talks with the Lord regularly. He hears the voice of God speaking in the Bible. He cultivates fellowship with other believers. He leans on the Lord for strength to conquer sin. This kind of a relationship is called "abiding in Christ."[19] Without the Savior we can do nothing — not even get along with our spouses![20] But through him we can do everything, even to the point of making our homes all that he wants them to be![21]

---

[18]Psalm 18:30a.    [19]John 15:4, KJV.    [20]John 15:5.    [21]Philippians 4:13.

# CHAPTER FOUR

# GROW UP!

Many marriage counselors are convinced that one of the greatest obstacles to a successful marriage is selfishness. To be selfish is to be excessively concerned with one's own welfare, advantage, or pleasure without regard for others. Babies are notoriously selfish. They are oblivious to anything but their own well-being. When they are uncomfortable they scream until someone relieves their discomfort. Their disposition is determined by the degree to which things go their way.

We expect babies to gradually mature — physically, intellectually, and emotionally. Unfortunately, while many people mature physically and intellectually, their emotional growth lags far behind. They still view the world as they did when they were babies. They see it as a huge sphere revolving around themselves, existing primarily for their own well-being. They never really grow from egocentricity to a consideration of others. When things do not go their way they react in some infantile way, such as by crying, pouting, pitying themselves, throwing a temper tantrum, or even throwing objects near at hand. They may try to attract attention to themselves by boasting of their accomplishments or criticizing others.

If we place two babies together without supervision they usually encounter problems in a hurry! Likewise, an emotionally immature man and an emotionally immature woman who have become united in marriage are sure to undergo conflicts. Emotional babies don't make very good marriage partners! One of the greatest needs for stable and successful marriages is maturity.

Maturity is basically unselfishness. Of course, no human being is totally unselfish; there is a little immaturity in all of us. Someone has said, "Scratch an adult and you'll find a child." Someone else has suggested that the only difference between a man and a boy is that a man's toys cost more! Since no one is perfectly mature, it becomes obvious that maturity is a relative term rather than an absolute one. In fact, maturity is a process rather than a fixed condition.

A certain degree of emotional maturity is possible even for unbelievers, since the sin nature has areas of strength as well as areas of weakness. You may know some non-Christians who are quite unselfish in certain areas of their lives, as with their spouses, their children, their relatives, or their in-laws. They may be extremely gracious and kind toward neighbors, business associates, or people in the community. They may show great compassion toward the needy and underprivileged. But when you get to know them well, you will usually find that they also have glaring areas of immaturity and selfishness.

When a person accepts Jesus Christ as his personal Savior, another factor is introduced into his life. In addition to his sinful ego, with its strengths and weaknesses, the Lord Jesus Christ indwells him in the Person of his Holy Spirit. A person's entire disposition now depends upon whether self or the Spirit is in control. Since the Holy Spirit is the only Person who can keep every expression of self in control, our relationship with him becomes the single most important factor in our progressive development. We refer to this development as spiritual maturity rather than merely as emotional maturity. The two are similar, except that while emotional maturity relates primarily to the development of our human personality, spiritual maturity also recognizes the presence of the Holy Spirit in our lives and relates to our growing relationship with him.

We have learned that a Christian is either spiritual or carnal to the degree that the Holy Spirit or his own sinful flesh controls his life. It is interesting to note that the Apostle Paul compares carnality to babyhood. He wrote to the Corinthians "as unto carnal, even as unto babes."[1] The reason some Christians act immaturely is because their fleshly natures are in control of their lives. In other words, they are carnal. Since there is a parallel between carnality and immaturity, we can assume that there is also a parallel between spirituality and maturity. The spiritual Christian shows evidence of growing up, of spiritual adulthood.

Even a new believer can be relatively mature. We sometimes refer to a very young child as being mature for his age. We mean that he is showing unusual evidences of development. Maturity involves growth, and we are to continue growing spiritually throughout our Christian lifetime.[2] There is no such thing as sinless perfection in this life — simply continuing growth.

Spiritual growth takes place only as the Holy Spirit controls our lives. As we submit to him, he takes charge of more and more specific areas of our lives; we thus become increasingly capable of building a happy marital relationship. Let us examine several specific characteristics of maturity.

1) *A mature person accepts himself as God made him.* He feels neither inferior over his shortcomings nor egotistical about his strengths. He knows that his body, his brains, and his abilities were given to him by God for God's own purposes.[3] He is therefore neither inflated with pride over his successes nor unduly discouraged by his failures. A serious inferiority complex can produce tremendous tension in a marriage. A person who demands constant reassurance to bolster his sagging ego can drive his spouse to distraction. Likewise, a haughtier-than-thou egotist who contantly belittles his mate to enhance himself can produce the same tragic effect. Both reactions are childish, but God will help a person overcome them if he willingly depends on the indwelling Spirit. When a Christian learns to accept himself humbly for what he is as God

---

[1] 1 Corinthians 3:1, KJV.  [2] 2 Peter 3:18.  [3] Psalm 139:13-16; Romans 9:20; 1 Corinthians 4:7.

made him, he will soon learn to accept others as they are too, and that will constitute a giant step toward establishing a happy home.

2) *A mature person profits by his mistakes and by the suggestions of others.* Immature people try to find excuses for their failures. They blame them on other people or on God. When they are criticized, they take it as a personal affront, striking back with an angry defense like, "Well, you're not so great, either!" Emotional babies are more concerned about protecting their own egos than in growing. On the other hand, a mature person graciously accepts criticism, honestly evaluating his life in the light of God's Word and depending on the Holy Spirit to bring about the desired changes. He sees suggestions from other people as a part of God's plan for bringing him to maturity.

Such an attitude will help relieve another area of tension in marriage. Instead of reacting to some suggestion with, "You never appreciate anything I do," the mature person will say something like, "Thank you for your suggestion, Dear. With the Lord's help, I'll try to improve that." Of course, the mature person will also be careful how he makes suggestions. He will wait for the proper time, maintain an attitude of love and appreciation, and accompany his suggestion with words of commendation and encouragement.

3) *A mature person adjusts to things he cannot change.* One of the most practical prayers ever uttered was, "Lord, give me strength to change what can be changed, grace to accept what cannot be changed, and wisdom to know the difference!" It is an unhappy fact that while most married couples love each other, many marriage partners simply cannot stand the little idiosyncrasies which they see in their spouses; they thus continually try to change their mates. Those irritating habits seem to send them into orbit, and as they allow the faults to prey on their minds they soon lose sight of the fine qualities that attracted them in the first place. The result is a deep-

ening bitterness that destroys not only their marriages but their own personal lives as well. This is both childish and sinful.[4] The fruit of the Spirit is longsuffering; that is, a willingness to bear patiently with the provoking traits in others. The Holy Spirit will produce that grace in us if we will let him.

Some people who cannot accept reality flee to the unreal world of wishes and imagination. When the cold fact dawns on them that the person they married is not the matinee idol they created in their minds, they withdraw sullenly into a world of dreams, thereby crushing all hopes of improving the relationship. Mature Christians, on the other hand, find their deepest satisfaction in the Lord.[5] They are thus able to accept the real world and the people in it as part of God's plan for helping them grow.

4) *A mature person accepts unpleasantness, disappointment, or distress with calmness and stability.* He recognizes that his life is in God's hands — that everything God allows is purposeful and good.[6] The mature person therefore maintains his self-control when things do not go his way. There is calmness and control when a husband brings home news of a transfer to some far-off city or when a wife calls the office to say she ran into the rear of another car!

Sometimes the tiniest things irritate us and cause us to act selfishly and immaturely. One survey showed that the most common complaint of husbands and wives against each other is an irritable disposition. We let trivial things "get to us" and upset us; then we react either by losing our tempers or by clamming up and pouting. In the course of my marriage counseling I have heard some fantastic accounts of immature behavior among professing Christians, such as husbands who threw objects around the house or others who hit their wives and shoved them around. I learned of one man who lay on the floor and kicked and screamed like a baby, and of another who put his fist through the wall in an angry rage over

---

[4]Ephesians 4:31.    [5]Psalm 73:25.    [6]Psalm 18:30a; 31:15; 37:23; Romans 8:28.

something his wife had done! If our marriages are ever to glorify God, we need to grow up by allowing the Holy Spirit to take control of our lives. He will then display through us his fruit of self-control.

Though the preceding examples mentioned only husbands, the wives are by no means guiltless. I have listened to husbands describe kicking and screaming wives or, more commonly, moody and unpredictable mates. There is nothing more discouraging for a husband than to come home after a taxing day at work to find his wife stewing and churning about some petty aggravation which poisons the family atmosphere throughout the entire evening. Solomon must have had this experience. "A dry crust eaten in peace is better than steak every day along with argument and strife."[7] "Better to live in the desert than with a quarrelsome, complaining woman."[8] "A nagging wife annoys like constant dripping."[9] The continuous dripping of water was a form of oriental torture — not a very flattering simile! Irritability becomes a way of life, a habit pattern. We need to yield to the Holy Spirit and grow up.

5) *A mature person accepts and fulfills his responsibilities.* Maturity involves dependability. Unfinished jobs, broken promises, and unfulfilled good intentions are examples of *un*dependability. An immature person cannot happily perform the tasks for which he is responsible. He grumbles and complains, finding no satisfaction or enjoyment in a job well done. Housewives grumble because life is dull and routine. Working mothers long to be full-time homemakers. Men hop from job to job in quick, haphazard decisions that fail to include their wives. Some men overlook the common courtesy of phoning their wives when they cannot come home at the expected time. The fruit of the Spirit is faith, a word meaning "faithfulness" or "dependability." We need to yield to the Spirit and grow up to faithfulness!

[7]Proverbs 17:1, TLB.    [8]Proverbs 21:19, TLB.    [9]Proverbs 19:13, TLB.

6) *A mature person finds his greatest satisfaction in making others happy.* We will never find happiness by simply looking for it. The more we look, the more frustrated and disappointed we become. Selfishly seeking our own enjoyment yields nothing but unhappiness. Unselfishly living for the good of others brings rich returns, a lesson which most marriage partners still need to learn. When we trust the Spirit of God to make us so unselfish that we live solely for the happiness of our mates, asking for no favors in return, the enjoyment we receive will be unbelievably abundant. Every time you trigger a conflict in your marriage relationship, ask yourself, "Now why did I do that?" You'll probably have to admit that you did it for your own enjoyment or convenience. Apologize and redirect your words or acts for the good of your mate. Do not even imply that your mate should do the same. Before long you may discover that your mate is responding with a new consideration too!

Now this costs something. In fact, it costs everything. But mature people are willing to give everything, then patiently wait for the Lord to work. It is only babies and children who demand *what* they want *when* they want it. They live for the here and now, insisting on their own way in every situation. Mature people often forego immediate personal pleasures so they can bring ultimate enjoyment to others. Paradoxically, this is what brings genuine happiness to the giver, too!

This vital lesson takes time to learn. We all feel we have a right to indulge our selfishnesses occasionally. We've been doing it for years, so why change now! But the more frequently we respond to situations in the control of the Holy Spirit, the easier the practice will become and the more quickly we will mature. "When I was a child, I spoke as a child, I understood as a child, I thought as a child; but when I became a man, I put away childish things."[10]

[10] 1 Corinthians 13:11, KJV.

# CHAPTER FIVE

# I'M IN LOVE

Love is a popular subject today. Never before in history have we heard so much about it yet seen so little of it in action. Often we use the word rather loosely. For instance, a person may say he loves his family, his new car, or even pepperoni pizza! Hardly anyone specifies the kind of love he means. Newspapers have been known to headline "love murders" or "love suicides" — a rather strange concept indeed! It is obvious that the word "love" means different things to different people. Yet love is a foundational concept in the Christian gospel as well as the single most important ingredient in a successful marriage. We therefore ought to find out what love really means.

In the last chapter we spoke of spiritual maturity. It is not by accident that we selected love as our next subject, for both concepts are closely related. Like maturity, love is a process rather than a state. People don't actually "fall in love"; they grow into it instead. Maturing love involves growing from a state of receiving much and giving little toward a state of cheerfully giving everything and demanding nothing in return. This whole process is a part of maturity.

A baby must be loved or it will die. It receives love, but it has none to give in return. The cuddling which mothers interpret as an expression of love is really only the baby's intuitive effort to get food and gratify self. Newborn babies love only themselves. As the baby grows, however, he becomes more aware of his mother. She cares for him, feeds him, and provides companionship for him through most of his waking hours. This new awareness involves growth and development. A child's first expressions of affection will therefore usually be directed to his mother.

Soon the father comes into view, and the child's world broadens to include this new authority figure. Later he begins to reach out to brothers and sisters, then to playmates (usually of his own age and sex). Soon he'll want to be in a gang of his peers, most of whom will probably idolize some hero of their own sex. Then he explodes into adolescence, and peers of the opposite sex are no longer dreaded enemies but attractive and alluring friends. One day the announcement is made, "I'm in love." Is it really love? What has happened? What is love?

As you probably know, the Greeks had at least three different words for love, each describing a different aspect or level of love. Since we have only one word for love in English, we will face some degree of confusion in interpreting the biblical uses of the Greek words unless we learn the distinctiveness of each.

The first word, *eros,* is found in secular Greek literature but is never used in the Bible itself. *Eros* is totally human love. It often refers to sexual love, as the English word "erotic" implies. The basic idea in *eros* is getting something for yourself. While it may involve a genuine feeling for someone else, that feeling is kindled by the attractiveness of that person and by the excitement, pleasure, and satisfaction which we believe that person will afford us. *Eros* poses as love for another but is actually love for oneself. It says, "I love you because you make me happy." Its foundation is some characteristic in the other person that pleases us, such as beauty, charm, warmth, kindness, or talent. If that characteristic is taken away there is nothing left, and it dies. This kind of love looks primarily for what it can get. It may give a little, but the motive is usually to get something in return for what it gives. If it fails to get what it wants, it may turn to resentment, bitterness, or hatred.

Unfortunately, many young people choose a life partner on the basis of *eros*. Emotional involvement based on body chemistry reaches its full potential very rapidly, and the intensity of the *eros* causes it to be misconstrued as genuine love. The couple may know very little about each other, but they insist that their love will carry them through. Unfortunately, it usually doesn't, since it was never true love in the first place. The romantic bubble bursts when the "ideal" person turns out to be far less than ideal — thoughtless, rude, unromantic, unattentive, and unshaven! Since neither partner will be getting what he expected, both will probably want to call it quits, and another marital disaster will be added to the towering pile.

It is my practice to interview couples who ask me to marry them, and then to provide the premarital counsel which I deem appropriate. If some glaring problem is uncovered, I endeavor to deal with it to the best of my ability. After talking to Dave and Betty I had serious misgivings about marrying them at all. It became obvious that Dave's main desire in marriage was the gratification of physical desires. Betty was closing her eyes to this because of her determination to escape an unpleasant situation at home and because of the flattery she felt from Dave's attentions.

In a private session with Betty I warned her as tactfully as I could against marrying immediately. Maybe time would help them understand each other better and bring things to the surface that should be dealt with before the pressures of marriage complicated them. And certainly if Dave loved Betty he would be willing to wait a little while for her. But Betty became indignant and told Dave of my insinuations. They decided to have nothing more to do with me, and instead asked someone else to marry them. I lost touch with Dave and Betty after that, but subsequently I learned that two years and two children later Betty was a divorcee, struggling to finish her education while providing for her children. *Eros* had failed to sustain their relationship.

Unfortunately, it isn't easy to avoid a pitfall like this, for our whole culture is geared to convincing us that *eros* is love, that being loved is more important than loving, and that being loved depends on being attractive. So we buy suits, dresses, hair spray, toothpaste, mouthwash, makeup, deodorant, and other assorted aids to make us more attractive, so that hopefully someone will fall in love with us and make us happy. This exaggerated emphasis on *eros* accounts for a large percentage of all broken marriages.

The "Playboy philosophy" is *eros* in action. It holds that a woman is an attractive plaything for a man's gratification and pleasure, and that sexual approaches are synonymous with "making love." But love is more than sex. No relationship built on the physical alone can last very long, for physical desires are subject to satiation and loss of interest. When this occurs, the relationship will begin to deteriorate rapidly unless an intimacy of spirit and soul has also developed.

Marriages established only on *eros* will probably experience difficulties from the start. The courtship and engagement periods should instead be used to establish communion of spirit and soul. Then the physical union after marriage will be the crowning glory of a growing relationship rather than the worn-out link of a decaying relationship. If you made the dreadful mistake of marrying on the basis of *eros* alone, however, there is some encouraging news for you. Love can grow. It won't grow automatically, but it will grow if you cultivate it. The only hope for your marriage is to move on to higher levels of love.

*Philia,* the next higher level of love, relates to the soul rather than to the body. It touches the human personality — the intellect, the emotions, and the will. It involves a mutual sharing. The closest word in English would probably be "friendship." While the noun form is used only once in the New Testament,[1] the verb "to love, to like" and the adjective, "loving, devoted" are used many times. This is the degree of affection which Peter claimed for Christ when

[1]James 4:4.

the Lord asked, "Peter, do you love me?" Peter responded, "You know that I like you," or "You know that I'm your friend."[2]

There is some *eros* in *philia*. We choose friends because of the pleasure we derive from being with them. There are personal qualities in them that we appreciate, intellectual and cultural interests that we share, and mutual self-expression that we find satisfying. We derive something enjoyable from the relationship, but we are also willing to give our fair share. This giving is not free from selfish motivation, but the selfishness is largely obscured by a sense of togetherness. *Philia* is a higher level of love than *eros* in that "our" happiness is involved rather than merely "my" happiness.

Many comparatively happy marriages are built on *philia*. In fact, it is a good idea if a husband and wife *are* friends. I know some husbands and wives who say they love each other but aren't even friends! They really do not seem to enjoy each other's company. A marriage cannot survive unless love has grown at least to the *philia* level. If you are a young person contemplating marriage, you should take the time to discover whether you truly like the person with whom you intend to join yourself for life. A few months is not long enough to learn the little faults and shortcomings that might irritate and exasperate you after marriage. You have heard that love is blind, but in reality only *eros* is blind. It closes its eyes to faults, laughs off shortcomings, and rationalizes potential problems. *Philia,* on the other hand, honestly faces all these things and decides whether they are overshadowed by contrasting strengths. If they are, *philia* determines to live cheerfully with the weaknesses in the everyday give-and-take of life.

*Philia* is love's halfway mark — give a little, get a little; a fifty-fifty proposition. A couple can make it on this kind of love as long as each one does his part and the circumstances of life remain fairly steady. If one partner fails to contribute his share, however, or

[2]John 21:15, 16.

if unusual stress is introduced (financial crisis, serious illness, in-law tensions, sexual problems, child-rearing problems, etc.), the friendship suffers. *Philia* can't take the strain. It finally becomes selfish and demanding, and comradeship turns to conflict. The only hope for stable, successful, fully satisfying marriages is to grow to the highest level of love.

That level of love is *agape*. It does not seek pleasure for itself, but instead delights in giving. It is not kindled by the merit or worth of its object, but originates in its own God-given nature. *Agape* keeps on loving even when its object is unresponsive, unkind, unlovable, or completely unworthy. It desires only the good of the one loved. It lives to make the loved one happy, whatever the personal cost or sacrifice. It doesn't give fifty percent and expect fifty percent in return. It gives one hundred percent and expects nothing in return!

Watch out for counterfeits! Some will try to give this kind of love in order to get more love in return. It may appear to work this way, but that is not the motive of true *agape*. Some may try to give pseudo-*agape* because they enjoy the ego-satisfaction of being considered benevolent or of having someone dependent on them. True *agape* is totally unselfish and uncalculating.

You say, "But that's not even human." You're right! No human being in the world can originate true *agape*. *Agape* is given by God alone. In fact, God himself is *agape*.[3] The Bible is filled with descriptions of God giving, sacrificing, and providing for sinners like ourselves.[4] When we receive Jesus Christ as our Savior, God pours his *agape* into our inner being: "We feel this warm love everywhere within us because God has given us the Holy Spirit to fill our hearts with his love."[5] God's love is then displayed in our daily experience.

But how do we actually display the love of God? We know we need this kind of love in our homes if we want them to be truly Christian and genuinely happy, but we simply do not seem to be able

[3] 1 John 4:8.   [4] cf. John 3:16; Romans 5:8; 1 John 3:16; 4:10.   [5] Romans 5:5, TLB.

to give it. Instead, we display an insatiable hunger to be loved, a craving which psychologists say is basic to human living. We try every means we can think of to get the love we crave, but most of our efforts only backfire and further alienate the one whose love we seek. We've learned by bitter experience that we cannot make someone love us.

The solution is found in God's Word. "We love him because he first loved us."[6] God's love for us generates love in our own hearts. Is your heart filled with bitterness, resentment, or hard feelings? God loves you, just as you are, in spite of your sinful, selfish attitudes and acts. *God loves you!* Contemplate his love, enjoy his love, revel in his love, drink deeply of his love, thank him for his love. The wonder of it all may make your sins even more hideous and vile in your own eyes, but you will confess them, and in love he will forgive and cleanse you, and the wonder of his forgiving love will overwhelm you even more. Soon you will find yourself abandoning your entire being to him, letting him fill and control you, letting him live his life through you. Then real love, *agape,* will flow through you to those around you, for the fruit of the Spirit is *agape.*[7] The result will be a new you, one who knows how to love in the highest and noblest sense of the word.

Our motive for this transformation should not be to change those around us, but this will nevertheless be the effect over a period of time. The principle we have just discovered from God's Word is that love produces love. Other passages teach the same truth. "A man will always reap just the kind of crop he sows!"[8] When we sow love we reap love. "If you give, you will get!"[9] When we give love we will receive love. We need to open our hearts to the love of God and let him express his love through us to our partners in marriage. He will use it to transform our marriages into the beautiful relationships he planned them to be.

[6] 1 John 4:19, KJV.    [7] Galatians 5:22.    [8] Galatians 6:7, TLB.    [9] Luke 6:38, TLB.

# CHAPTER SIX

# "BUT THE GREATEST OF THESE..."

The most important element in a happy Christian home is love, but what many people *think* is love is really not the highest form of love at all. It is either *eros,* a feeling inspired by something attractive in its object, or *philia,* a sense of comradeship and friendship. These sentiments can sustain a relationship for awhile and may even bring a degree of happiness, but if a couple aspires to an abundant and abiding joy in marriage they will need *agape,* God's kind of love. *Agape* does not grasp after what it can get, but pursues only what it can give, and it keeps giving even when it gets nothing in return.

When the Holy Spirit controls our lives and expresses *agape* through us, certain elements of *eros* and *philia* will still be present in our marital relationships. We will still appreciate the attractiveness of our loved ones and the physical expressions of love with them. We will derive great satisfaction from a sense of togetherness, an intimacy of mind, emotions, and will. But our love will no longer depend on the attractiveness of our mates, nor will the continuous expression of our love depend on the pleasure we experience. The source of our ever-growing love will be God himself. He sanctifies the *eros* and *philia* and makes them meaningful and precious. Life becomes balanced and beautiful, and God's happiness reigns supreme in our homes.

What is a home like when the husband and wife are both filled with the Spirit, and *agape* is being expressed? The answer is found in First Corinthians 13, the great love chapter. Every occurrence of the word "charity" or "love" in this chapter translates the Greek word *agape.* The chapter actually contains a *description* of love rather than a definition; it shows us how *agape* acts. Though true *agape* applies to every object of love, such as God himself, other believers, our children, or a lost world, we are going to confine our application in this chapter to the husband-wife relationship.

1) "Love suffers long." It is long-tempered, slow to anger, slow to take offense, slow to become resentful. True love causes us to bear patiently with our loved ones when they wrong us, offend us, nag us, or criticize us. It is slow to assert itself or to retaliate in self-defense. The one who loves is willing to be a doormat if necessary, to let his loved one walk all over him without retaliation, self-pity, or sarcastic retorts.

Some will reply, "That's not love; that's a one-way street to Ulcerville. I'd have a nervous breakdown if I did that." On the contrary, that is the way we show our loved ones that we really do love them; when they are convinced of this fact they will begin to respond in like manner, for love produces love. To insist on our rights and to strike back when we are wronged will only prolong the conflict, and it is this prolonged irritation that produces ulcers and breakdowns. We cannot afford *not* to be doormats if that is what our situations demand. Some will protest, "But you don't know my husband/wife; he/she will keep on taking advantage of me, walking all over me and enjoying it." But wait a moment. Are you questioning the inspired Word of the eternal God? "Give and it shall be given unto you." "Whatever a man soweth, that shall he also reap." "We love him because he first loved us." Trust God to do what he says he will do. Keep on expressing his patient love, whatever the consequences, for he promises that ultimately it will bring you genuine love in return.

2) "Love is kind." This is the positive side of the first principle. Patience refrains from reacting to provocation, while kindness finds constructive ways of doing good for the ones we love no matter how they have acted. Kindness is showing appreciation for little things, looking for things we like and saying so with sincere com-

mendation. Some husbands or wives cannot recall the last compliment they received from their spouses.

Kindness is a helping hand, and that goes for husbands as well as wives. Kindness is a tone of voice, an approving look or smile. Some husbands and wives seldom speak kindly to each other. They know how to speak in pleasant tones to other people, but they growl at each other. Try the kindness check at your house for awhile. Whenever you say something to your mate that elicits a negative response, ask yourself, "Was that kind?" If it wasn't, confess it to God, apologize to your mate, and trust God for the grace to be kind. It may work wonders in your marriage.

3) "Love envies not." Love is not jealous; it is not in competition with its loved one, nor is it hurt when it comes out second best. Unfortunately, husbands and wives are sometimes jealous of each other. The husband may be jealous of his wife's talents, her leadership abilities, her capacity for getting along with other people, or her understanding of God's Word. The wife may be jealous of the time her husband spends with the children, or the attention the children give him when he comes home from work — after she has given of herself all day to care for them. She may be jealous of the time and effort the husband gives to his job, to the church, or to something else he enjoys. Either of them may feel surges of jealousy when some member of the opposite sex seems especially friendly to their spouse. *Agape* love is not possessively jealous, and does not insist on having all the attention all the time.

4) "Love vaunts not itself, is not puffed up." These two ideas are similar to each other. To vaunt means to brag or boast. To be puffed up is to be arrogant and conceited. Love is not inflated; it does not carry an exaggerated estimate of its own importance. It does not consider itself superior to its object. Pride is extremely subtle, whether it be pride over superior ability, better education,

higher refinement, greater spirituality, or any one of a number of things. It creeps in unnoticed, but it is almost always reflected in our attitude toward our mates, eating away at our relationship until there is little left.

Sometimes we feel that we have been unusually sweet or have done something particularly wonderful. We long to be complimented, but the compliment never comes. Our feelings become hurt, and we start to rehearse what we've done in order to get the praise we crave. This is not love, for love does not boast. It may have been a lack of love that withheld the compliment in the first place, but each of us will answer to God for ourself — not for our mate.

5) "Love does not behave itself unseemly." Love is never unmannerly, but always acts courteously and politely. When we truly love, we make the effort to do little things that show how much we care. Whoever it was that said, "Chivalry is dead" spoke a mouthful. Most wives find that their husbands seldom open car doors for them anymore or practice other simple acts of propriety that show loving consideration. The husbands are not the only guilty ones, however. Some wives react indignantly when their husbands make reasonable requests in pleasant tones. Others demonstrate a gross lack of courtesy by interrupting their husbands when they are speaking. Love is never rude.

6) "Love seeks not her own." Here is the very essence of love — unselfishness, the absence of all self-seeking. Love does not insist on its own way or on its own rights. The matter of violated rights is probably one of the most common trouble spots in shaky marriages. All of us believe that we have certain inalienable rights: the right to be appreciated, the right to have certain things our way, the right to enjoy certain personal comforts, the right to have our needs met. When our spouses violate these rights, we react with anger and indignation. But true biblical meekness is the willingness to give up

our rights for the people we love. Actually, when we yield ourselves fully to God, we happily surrender all of our rights to him. If we have honestly given all of them to him, we have none left to be violated! We will gratefully enjoy only those rights which the Lord sees fit to restore to us in his own good pleasure. Think back to some conflict with the one you profess to love, and you will probably uncover some right of yours that you felt was violated. When you are tempted to demand your right, ask God for the grace and power to leave it with him. Then watch the tensions begin to ease in your marriage relationship.

7) "Love is not easily provoked." It is neither touchy nor irritable. Since it has surrendered all its rights for the one it loves, it has nothing to get upset about. Love is not easily aroused to anger, doesn't wear its feelings on its sleeve, is not temperamental. Touchy people make poor marriage partners; they need to let the Spirit of God give them victory in this area of their lives if they hope to find happiness in marriage.

8) "Love thinks no evil." Love does not dwell on the wrongs it has suffered from the object of its love. Neither does it magnify human faults. Love forgives and forgets; it doesn't hold grudges or tabulate grievances! Have you ever thought back over your married life and enumerated the many times you have been wronged? We are particularly inclined to do this when we are building a case for a good argument. But that is not love. Have you ever let your mind dwell on all the faults and shortcomings of your mate until you felt shortchanged? We are especially prone to do this after a heated or prolonged argument. But this is not love either. "Thinking no evil" likewise eliminates the continual criticism and disapproval to which some husbands and wives subject their mates. It will take Spirit-empowered discipline to stop this dreadful habit if you have already fallen into it, but you will discontinue it if you really love. A good

place to begin might be to write out a list of your mate's good points. Read it every time you are tempted to find fault. The Lord may use it to change your attitude dramatically.

9) "Love rejoices not in iniquity, but rejoices in the truth." This statement alludes to that sinister satisfaction which we sometimes feel when someone who has injured us is caught doing something wrong. "He only got what he deserved" is our heartless reaction. The verse may also refer to those occasions when we gloat over the shortcomings of our mates in a selfish attempt to vindicate ourselves. For example, we may still be smarting over some critical word spoken by our mate when suddenly he does something obviously wrong. We capitalize on the situation with some comment like, "See, you're not so perfect either!" Love does not rejoice when wrong is done, but when truth and right prevail.

10) "Love bears all things." The word translated "bear" means literally "to cover, to pass over in silence, to keep confidential." Love does not broadcast the faults of its object. It does not belittle the one it professes to love by exposing his shortcomings and failures in the presence of other people. While this is the favorite indoor sport of some married couples, it is not love. Love keeps these things confidential.

11) "Love believes all things." This does not mean that love is gullible, but that it is beyond suspicion, doubt, and mistrust. True love eliminates the third degree: "Where were you? What were you doing? Who were you with? Why couldn't you get home sooner?" Some women protest when they hear that love believes all things. "But he's lied to me so many times; I just can't believe him anymore." Maybe you can't believe *him,* but you can believe that God will use your love for him and your trust in him to change his life. Love keeps on believing.

12) "Love hopes all things." Love does not magnify problems

in order to justify quitting. Love never gives up hope, never despairs. It just keeps on going.

13) "Love endures all things." The concept is that of sustaining an assault. Love weathers every storm of suffering or persecution. It takes every blow and still keeps coming back for more — cheerfully!

14) "Love never fails." It never falls to pieces, never collapses, never terminates. As long as the Spirit of God is in control of our lives he just keeps on producing love and we just keep on displaying it! If we ever stop, we will know that the Spirit of God is no longer in control, for his love never ends.

I wish you could hear Karen describe how the Word of God worked in her life. Her husband, Bruce, had grown up in the church and had professed Christ as his Savior at an early age, but he had never evidenced much spiritual reality in his behavior. After Karen and Bruce were married things went from bad to worse. Bruce began drinking heavily, staying out most of the night, squandering their money, and mistreating Karen and the children.

As the days dragged into years the situation continued to deteriorate. Karen's friends begged her to leave Bruce for the sake of the children and for her own physical and mental well-being. However, she refused, for she was confident that God would change her husband. She had surrendered her right to enjoy a loving and considerate husband, and had asked God to fill her with greater love and kindness in spite of the cruelty she was enduring. She kept on believing and hoping.

It was several years later that I sat in their living room and listened to their story. Bruce was now a dependable husband and father and a spiritual leader at home and in church. "To what do you attribute the change?" I asked. "There were several factors," he replied. "The Lord used a visiting evangelist to clinch the decision. But the greatest single influence was Karen — her willingness to stick with me and put up with all the misery I caused her. I knew she really loved me. It was that love that brought me to my senses."

The Apostle Paul concluded his magnificent discourse on love by listing three great Christian virtues — faith, hope, and love. It should come as no surprise to us that his very last statement is, "But the greatest of these is love."[1] This *agape* — this love of God — is the greatest thing in the world. It can revolutionize our homes and make them into everything we ever dreamed they could be. But it all depends on us — on our willingness to allow God's Spirit to produce this phenomenon of love in our hearts and lives.

[1] 1 Corinthians 13:13.

# CHAPTER SEVEN

# THIS IS A GREAT MYSTERY

Men and women are different! You may consider this rather self-evident, but the differences are really important to consider, since the trend of our day is to minimize the differences, magnify the likenesses, and pervert the meaning of equality. We hear that women can do anything men can do, and some women are fighting for men's jobs to prove it. Clothing styles tend to obscure the differences between the sexes. The biblical order of authority in the home is mocked by modern sociologists. Modern brides want the word "obey" taken out of their wedding ceremonies because they think it reduces them to the status of a slave.

God made men and women to be different. "Male and female created he them."[1] "At the beginning God created man and woman."[2] Men and women walk differently, talk differently, think differently, and even eat differently! They are motivated by different values and are affected by different emotions. They differ in every cell of their bodies.

While there are varying degrees of difference between various men and women, including exceptions to almost every generalization, we can nevertheless enumerate several important differences. Generally speaking, men are stronger physically than women. They are guided more by logic than are women, who seem to rely a great deal on intuition and emotion. Men are usually more objective, women more subjective. Men are often realistic, women idealistic. Many men are self-assured, while women frequently need reassurance. Men seem to be more rigid in their thinking, while women are often more adaptable and thus more susceptible to the influence of others. At the same time, women are generally more sympathetic than men. They seem to be especially interested in people, while

---

[1]Genesis 1:27, KJV.  [2]Matthew 19:4, TLB.

men are more interested in things. In the chapters to come we are going to explore some of these differences and the special needs they produce. We will see how God's specific instructions to husbands and wives are designed to help each partner meet the special needs of his mate. For the moment, however, we would like to learn why God created men and women with such distinct differences.

The Apostle Paul gets to the heart of the reason in his Letter to the Ephesians. If there is one thing he wanted these folks to understand about marriage, it was that the husband-wife relationship can be compared to the relationship between Christ and his church. He repeated it three times in three successive verses.[3] Then, after speaking of a man being joined to his wife, he makes this amazing assertion: "This is a great mystery, but I speak concerning Christ and the church."[4] The marriage relationship was intended by God to be a living illustration of the relationship between Christ and his church. Although marriage was instituted in the Garden of Eden long before the church began, that union nevertheless anticipated the fact that God would someday form the church and ultimately present it to his Son as his bride. This is a great mystery, a divine truth hidden in ages past but now clearly revealed. Marriage is a magnificent drama, vividly portraying the relationship between Christ and the church.

In the marriage drama the players are husband and wife. Each has a role to depict. The husband portrays Christ and the wife represents the church. Nothing could be clearer than this in Scripture:

"For a husband is in charge of his wife in the same way Christ is in charge of his body the church. . . . So you wives must willingly obey your husbands in everything, just as the church obeys Christ. And you husbands, show the same kind of love

---

[3]Ephesians 5:23-25.    [4]Ephesians 5:32, KJV.

to your wives as Christ showed to the church when he died for her. . . ."[5]

Each player must be uniquely adapted to his role. One very important reason that God made men and women so unlike each other is that man portrays Christ and woman portrays the church in this divinely-designed object lesson.

Just as there is an order of authority in the Christ-church relationship, so there is an order of authority in the husband-wife relationship. One of the most hotly debated and fiercely denounced concepts in all the Bible is that ". . . the husband is the head of the wife, even as Christ is the head of the church."[6] This is the biblical doctrine of headship. Properly understood and practiced, it is not a grudging and distasteful plight but a gratifying and delightful privilege. Since this doctrine is part of God's infallible Word, there cannot be perfect harmony in marriage apart from its application. What, then, is headship?

Maybe we should decide first of all what it is *not*. Headship is not superiority. Nowhere does the Bible imply that men are superior to women. In fact, it clearly states that men and women are equal in God's sight. "There is neither male nor female; for ye are all one in Christ Jesus."[7] Two becoming "one flesh" would also seem to indicate equality. God created men and women equal, and women should be treated as equals — not as inferiors. Men who ridicule and belittle women probably do it to reassure their own manhood. If they can convince themselves that all men are superior to all women, then they feel superior to their wives no matter how weak or irresponsible they themselves might be!

Nor does headship consist of domination or dictatorship. The doctrine of headship does not destroy a wife's personality or will, nor does it reduce her to slave status. Actually it does just the opposite.

---

[5]Ephesians 5:23-25, TLB.   [6]Ephesians 5:23, KJV.   [7]Galatians 3:28, KJV.

Jesus Christ is the supreme example of headship, yet as the head of the church he ministers to it.[8] In this capacity Christ actually serves the church — a fact which we husbands need to think about! Some men have the false notion that headship means "I'm the boss and you'll do as I say whether you like it or not. Now get me my slippers."

Other men have the ridiculous idea that headship includes bullying rights. They get bullied at work by their bosses, so they come home and bully their wives and children to prove their masculinity. But brutality doesn't show masculinity. On the contrary, it shows weakness. The man who hits someone weaker than himself is demonstrating uncertainty about his actual strength. If he pushes his wife, drags her around, or strikes her, he is displaying his insecurity, immaturity, and incompetence as a husband. This kind of treatment puts wives in mental institutions. The man who thinks he can order his wife around like a slave is cheating her of a very wonderful privilege that God wants her to have.

On the positive side, headship is loving leadership. There is a universal need for leadership in every sphere of human experience. We have it in government — local, state, and federal. Our mayor, governor, and president are not necessarily superior to us, but as our duly chosen leaders they have delegated positional authority. We have authority in our schools, on our jobs, and in our churches.[9] We need to have it in our homes, too. The Bible declares, "But I would have you know that the head of every man is Christ, and the head of the woman is the man, and the head of Christ is God."[10] Probably the greatest example of headship to which we could point is that of God the Father as Head over God the Son. Christ has been equal with his Father from eternity past, yet he subjected himself to the authority of the Father. Just as the Father is the Head of

---

[8]Matthew 20:28.    [9]cf. 1 Thessalonians 5:12; 1 Timothy 5:17; Hebrews 13:17.
[10]1 Corinthians 11:3, KJV.

the Son and the Son is the Head of man, so man is the head of woman in the marital relationship.

The ladies are probably asking, "Why must this be so?" The answer is simple — to dramatize the submission of the church to the leadership of Jesus Christ. "But why must the woman take a *submissive* role?" Simply because of the way God made her. For one thing, she is physically weaker.[11] The weaker depends on the stronger, and the stronger leads the weaker. And so God said to Eve very early in her life, "He [Adam] shall be your master."[12] He was to be the head, with delegated positional authority.

The woman's God-given nature is to be led, to be dependent. She is not truly happy in any other role. Some women, because of selfishness or immaturity, seek to dominate their husbands — but they are not happier for the effort. The older such a woman gets and the more she realizes the extent to which she has weakened the man she married, the more she hates herself for it. The urge for a wife to nag, criticize, ridicule, belittle, or manipulate her husband may seem to be almost uncontrollable at times, but Jesus Christ can help her control it. She will never be happy unless she lets Christ transform her. God made a woman to lean on her husband; if she whittles him down to where he can no longer be leaned on, she is the one who suffers for it.

Unfortunately, some men shy away from their leadership role. With authority goes responsibility, demands, decisions, pressures, and much time. They have enough of these problems at work, and don't want to be bothered with more of them at home. Because they are more interested in their own convenience than in their biblical responsibilities, they force their wives into the leadership role — with chaotic results. This situation is contrary to the very nature of both man and woman as God made them. It brings friction, frustration, dissatisfaction, dissension, and discord. Gentlemen, take

[11] Peter 3:7.   [12] Genesis 3:16, TLB.

charge! Be the leader in your home. Take the initiative in making decisions, training the children, and establishing family worship. No man who shirks these obligations is qualified to be a leader in the church.[13]

One morning I asked fifty-one women in a ladies' Bible class what they needed most from their husbands. One lady replied, "I need him to assume headship and responsibility. I have to make decisions that he should make, and I don't enjoy wearing the pants." Many of the other women made similar comments. They were particularly concerned about their husbands' leadership in spiritual matters. Some professing Christian husbands refused to lead in prayer in their homes. Contrary to what women often say and do, deep down inside they do not want to dominate their husbands. They want to be lovingly led. This is the role which God has assigned them in the great drama of marriage.

How is this leadership implemented in the Christian home? I believe it is similar to the leadership exercised in any smoothly operating organization. No successful corporation can function properly with two heads. If there is a president and a vice-president, it is generally agreed that the president is the leader. The vice-president may actually be more brilliant than his boss, but the president still carries the greater authority. His status is not that of a dictator, but of a delegated authority. The arrangement will work best if there is a mutual confidence and trust between them, if they look to each other as equals, if each shares and contributes from his own abilities, resources, and experiences, and if they mold policies and make decisions by mutual consent, with both men abiding by those decisions after they are made. Behind it all, however, there is the realization that only one of them is actually the leader. In the last analysis it is he who is responsible for all that is done.

This is exactly how a Christian marriage should work. It could

[13]1 Timothy 3:4, 5.

be described as a democracy with male leadership. Each mate should be concerned for the other, and for the best interests of the marriage. There should be a mutual sharing in the making of decisions and the resolving of problems. Because each partner displays a genuine love for the other, irresolvable problems should be rare. But in those rare cases, God says that the husband lovingly leads and the wife lovingly follows.

This is God's blueprint for the Christian home. It is a long way from the perverted view that once considered women to be less than human. It is also a far cry from the equally dangerous modern philosophy which frees women from the responsibilities of the home, the kitchen, and the kids and liberates them from their husbands' authority.

A woman finds real equality and freedom when she assumes her God-given role as a helpmeet, relying on the man God has given her and graciously submitting to him. He in turn tenderly loves her, cherishes her, protects her, and provides for her. God planned the role of the man and the woman to dramatize the relationship between Christ and the church. He asks us to glorify him by accepting our roles willingly and fulfilling them faithfully.

# CHAPTER EIGHT

# WHAT EVERY HUSBAND NEEDS TO KNOW

There is a book in circulation entitled *What Men Know About Women*. Its pages are all blank! We have often heard some frustrated male sigh, "I'll never be able to understand women." Yet the Apostle Peter said, "Ye husbands, dwell with them according to knowledge."[1] This is a most amazing paradox. God tells men to dwell with their wives according to knowledge — an understanding of their basic nature and needs — but most men know very little about the makeup and mechanism of the female of the species. Could this be one of the reasons why so many marriages are floundering?

If God says that men are to live with their wives according to knowledge, then obviously they can know something about them, popular opinion notwithstanding! The first thing they need to know is stated in the very verse we have just quoted: "Giving honor unto the wife, as unto the weaker vessel." The woman is the weaker vessel. That doesn't mean she is mentally, morally, or spiritually inferior, but simply that she is *physically* weaker. She may be less susceptible to disease and may even have a longer lifespan than the man, but the fact remains that she is not as large or as strong physically. God made her that way with the intent that the weaker would depend on the stronger.

Because the wife is physically weaker, she depends on her husband for provision and protection. His task is to provide food, clothing, shelter, and defense, while she is especially adapted by God to bear children and to provide them with the warm affection and tender care which they need. However, the very equipment which God gave her to assume that role is likewise the cause of a second area of weakness — her emotions. A woman must some-

---

[1] 1 Peter 3:7, KJV.

times struggle with sudden and unexplainable changes in mood. These are chemically precipitated by hormones which form part of her reproductive capacity. This emotional vulnerability makes her especially dependent on the man God gives her. It seems to be the underlying idea in God's words to Eve: "You shall welcome your husband's affections."[2] She looks to him with an inner yearning to meet her basic needs. She was made for him, and so her life centers in him. God wants us husbands to "dwell with them according to knowledge," then act on the basis of that knowledge, "giving honor unto the wife, as unto the weaker vessel." The God who created these tremendous emotional needs in women intends that husbands should meet them.

Some of you may be asking, "What about women who have no husbands? Who will meet their needs?" God will bestow the gift of celibacy on those whom he intends to remain single. Furthermore, a woman's needs can be met by the Lord himself. In fact, every Christian woman, married or single, needs to maintain a close personal relationship with Christ. However, this does not excuse a husband from his responsibilities to his wife. God's normal way of supplying a married woman with the security and satisfaction for which she yearns is through her husband.

How does the husband do it? How can any man satisfy a woman's basic needs? This may sound like a gross oversimplification, but one little four-letter word is actually the complete answer to this entire complex problem. The husband's primary responsibility in a Christian marriage is to *love* his wife. "Husbands, love your wives, even as Christ also loved the church and gave himself for it."[3] "Husbands should [love] their wives . . . as parts of themselves."[4] "A man must love his wife as a part of himself."[5] "You husbands must be loving and kind to your wives, and not bitter against them."[6] All of these verses require *agape,* that highest level of love

---

[2]Genesis 3:16, TLB.   [3]Ephesians 5:25, KJV.   [4]Ephesians 5:28, TLB. [5]Ephesians 5:33, TLB.   [6]Colossians 3:19, TLB.

that keeps on giving even when it gets nothing in return and seeks only good for the one loved regardless of the personal cost or sacrifice.

This gives an entirely new meaning to the misunderstood doctrine of male headship. Headship is not some masculine doctrine cleverly designed to bolster the husband's sagging ego. Headship involves the husband's solemn obligation to establish an atmosphere of love in which the basic needs of his wife are fulfilled — an environment in which she is free to grow and develop into all that God wants her to be. Her submission will then be the voluntary response to his loving leadership.

The key word here is *response*. The woman is a responder. This is the obvious role of someone who depends on another person. Flowers depend on sunshine and rain; when they get it, they respond by blossoming into gorgeous beauty. This is how God made a woman, too. She responds to what she receives. If she receives irritability, criticism, disapproval, unkindness, indifference, lack of appreciation, or lack of affection, she will respond with a defense mechanism, such as bitterness, coolness, defiance, or nagging. Some women turn to drinking or submerge themselves in social activities.

But if the woman receives love she will respond with love, and will blossom into the most beautiful creature under God's heaven. When a man claims that his wife doesn't love him anymore he is unwittingly admitting that he hasn't loved her as he should have. If he had, she would most likely have responded with love in return. A man gets from his wife what he invests in her. He cannot force her to love him, but he can show love to her and enjoy her loving response. Thus the responsibility for a successful marriage rests initially with the husband. He makes the first move — that of loving his wife with the totally unselfish love of Jesus Christ.

"If she'd only quit nagging, I could love her more." If that's what you've been telling yourself, then you have it backwards! The husband must take the initiative. Love is a mental attitude which is received by an act of the human will from the source of all love, God himself. It does not depend on the worth or the actions of its object, but simply on the ceaseless love of a changeless Lord. A wife may be sweet or sour; the house may be clean or cluttered; supper may be tasty or terrible; but none of these should affect a husband's love. He is to love his wife "as Christ loved the church." We know all too well that Christ's love for the church wasn't prompted by anything wonderful he saw in us, but instead by his own intrinsic nature of love. Now he makes this same love available to every Christian husband who wants to make his marriage work.

"Husbands, love your wives as Christ also loved the church, and gave himself for it." Calvary, where Christ sacrifically gave himself, was the greatest demonstration of love in all of human history. Sacrificial self-giving is the very essence of love. Now God asks of every Christian husband the same self-giving love. That's important to remember — love gives. It will involve giving the material things a wife needs as finances permit, and perhaps even a little gift now and then that says, "I really care. I think about you when we're apart." It doesn't have to cost much money, but it does reassure a wife of her husband's love.

Love will also involve helping. Sometimes a husband develops the strange notion that his home is a castle and he is the king. His wife's task is to provide for his comfort and to protect him from all unpleasant circumstances. He rises majestically from dinner, sinks gloriously into his overstuffed chair, and entertains himself with the newspaper and television while his wife cleans up the kitchen, straightens up the house, helps the children with their homework, and puts them to bed. Any encroachment on his lordship's time is met with howls of protest. Most wives work hard, maybe even harder than their husbands, and no husband ought to be above helping with the housework and the children. If the wife is really the weaker vessel, then wiping the dishes, sweeping the floor, supervising the children, cleaning the windows, or dozens of other little helpful acts are just other ways of saying "I love you."

Self-sacrificing love will involve the giving of time. Some husbands are too busy to run an errand, fix a gadget, or devote an evening to their wives alone. They are saying in subtle little ways, "You're really not worth very much personal sacrifice," and this is like spraying weed killer on a beautiful flower. But when the wife begins to wilt and reflect the same attitude toward her husband, he is usually quick to complain about it. Problems like this will be solved when the husband begins to show the love of Christ.

Love may involve giving up things. Often a husband has interests or hobbies in which his wife finds no pleasure. Usually compromises can be made: she may develop special interests of her own, he may restrict his activities somewhat, or they may plan other special activities together. But if all reasonable attempts to solve the conflict fail, then God intends for the wife to know that she holds the most important place in her husband's life, that next to the Lord himself she is above everything and everyone. That does not give a wife the right to demand that her husband give up something to "prove his love," but it does lay upon every Christian husband the need for assuring his wife that he loves her above all else.

Christ-like love will involve reassurance and encouragement. Some men refuse to tell their wives that they love them. "I told her that when I married her, and she knows it's true." Yes, but a woman requires reassurance. Her whole life is wrapped up in the security of her husband's love, and the Lord wants her to be assured of it in every possible way. She needs to know that he cares — that he appreciates the things she does to please him, like maintaining his home and cooking his meals. She needs to know that he comes home because *she* is there — not just for meals and a bed! One of the most prevalent complaints of wives is that their husbands take them for granted, treating them as if they were maids. Here is what one woman said she needed most from her husband: "I need to feel needed, that what I am doing for him and for our children is important to him. Then, I want to be appreciated for the things I do." Most wives try hard to please, and they need to know that their husbands approve of their efforts and appreciate them.

Of all the things God wants a husband to give his wife, none is more important than what Christ gave — his own personal being. "Oh, I'd die to protect my wife," some would protest. Giving ourselves may not demand *dying* for our wives, but it certainly demands *living* for them, and that is the very thing many husbands are unwilling to do. They exclude their wives from their lives. They think working hard and providing an abundance of material things will make their wives happy. And while they are at work getting rich, their wives are at home with aching hearts, yearning to share their husbands' lives as God intended them to do, yearning for the appreciation, approval, attention, and affection which God intended them to have, yearning for the sympathetic understanding their God-given natures demand.

One woman wrote, "My husband needs to let me know that he is aware of my problems and understands them. I need to feel that we are working together toward a common goal." The one word that occurs most frequently when wives are discussing what they need from their husbands is *understanding*. No amount of material things can take the place of a husband who listens to his wife with undivided attention when she unfolds her heart, who tries to understand even her most complicated moods, and who lets her know that he loves her even during her most illogical and unreasonable moments.

That costs something; in fact, it costs everything. It demands total self-sacrifice. That is exactly what it cost Christ when his love led him to Calvary. If you are not willing to pay that cost, then you made a dreadful mistake when you promised a woman you would love her until death. God says she is part of you. You are one flesh.[7] She needs to be treated with the same loving care and concern with which you treat your own body. "So ought men to love their wives as their own bodies. He that loveth his wife loveth himself. For no man ever yet hated his own flesh, but nourisheth and cherisheth it, even as the Lord the church."[8] The word *nourish* means to supply the food and clothing which the body needs. The word *cherish* literally means to keep warm, but also includes the idea of tender, loving care, the kind of care a trained nurse would give to her own children.[9] Some men are like little boys; they want their wives to feed them when they are hungry and soothe them when they are hurt, just as their mothers did. Biblically, that comes closer to the role of the husband toward his wife than the role of the wife toward her husband.

Most men take pretty good care of their own bodies. They get plenty of food, proper rest, adequate clothing, a break from the monotonous routine, some enjoyable relaxation, some time to themselves, and a certain amount of personal satisfaction in life. But are they as interested in seeing that their wives get the same? They should be, according to the Word of God, because their wives are part of them. A man's care for his wife is, in effect, care for himself too, since both their lives are one.

That is exactly what Peter said in the verse with which we started this chapter: "You husbands must be careful of your wives, being thoughtful of their needs and honoring them as the weaker sex. Remember that you and your wife are partners in receiving God's blessings, and if you don't treat her as you should, your prayers will

---

[7]Ephesians 5:31.    [8]Ephesians 5:28, 29, KJV.    [9]1 Thessalonians 2:7.

not get ready answers."[10] When a man takes a woman to be his wife he makes her part of himself; he cannot afford to shut her out of his life. When he refuses to obey God's Word in this regard, a spirit of bitterness and resentment creeps into the marriage, spiritual power vanishes, and an effective prayer life is hindered. Much of the spiritual impotence of believers can be traced to this very matter. It's time for us to obey God's Word again!

On one occasion a Christian husband told me some of his wife's problems — a general discontentment, a proneness to pick and gripe at little things, and a constant irritability and unreasonableness. He had tried to improve himself in some areas in order to make her happy, but it was never enough. One day he blurted out, "That women will find something wrong with heaven!"

We discussed her immaturity and insecurity, much of which seemed to stem from her family background. But one day I suggested that all of her problems might not be traceable to her parents. Maybe some of them grew out of her God-given need to be reassured of his love. I asked him to do everything he could to make her feel more secure in his love. He accepted my challenge and with God's help began to make some changes.

He started to show his wife more affection, taking her in his arms as they passed in the house and telling her he loved her, even though it was not his natural inclination to be that demonstrative. He spent time with her away from the children, listening to her talk and making sympathetic comments. (He found that the best time to talk was while she was cleaning up the kitchen — the kids were nowhere to be found at that particular time!) He pitched in and helped while they talked. When she had had a bad day and got upset about some silly little thing that didn't please her, he asked God to keep him calm and help him assure her of his love at that very moment, instead of angrily defending himself and sulking, as he once had

[10] 1 Peter 3:7, TLB.

done. The transformation that gradually came over her was amazing. Their marriage isn't perfect as of this writing, but a woman who missed something very important in her childhood years is beginning to find in her husband the love that God intended her to have, and in that atmosphere of love she is growing into the beautiful person God planned for her to be.

Let me add just a brief word to wives. Let the indwelling Spirit of God motivate your husband in these matters. Don't try to do God's work for him. If you try to remake your husband yourself, the results will be far less than you hope for. It is not even your place to remind him of his responsibility. Instead, commit him to the Lord, pray for him, and be what God wants *you* to be.

# CHAPTER NINE

# WHAT EVERY WIFE NEEDS TO KNOW

The primary responsibility of the husband in a Christian home is to love his wife. This is mentioned a number of times in the Bible. In one passage of Scripture, however, wives are commanded to love their husbands.[1] While this one reference indicates that they are expected to help create an atmosphere of love in the home, their *primary* responsibility is introduced in the next verse, where they are exhorted to be ". . . obedient to their own husbands."[2] Obedience involves subjection and subordination. The word is used of the wife's responsibility to her husband no less than six times in the New Testament.[3]

We have discussed the subject of headship and God's order of authority in the home previously, but now we want to apply it specifically to the wife, for submission is her principal obligation. "You wives must submit to your husbands' leadership in the same way you submit to the Lord."[4] Ladies, submission to your husband is really submission to the Lord, because the Lord commands you to do it! If you cannot find it in you to submit to your husband for *his* sake, do it for the *Lord's* sake. The Lord loves you with a perfect love. Respond to his love with subjection to your husband.

"You wives must willingly obey your husbands in everything, just as the church obeys Christ."[5] Those two words "in everything" are rather broad, aren't they? Obedience is not to be practiced only when you feel like it, or when you wholeheartedly agree with your husband, or when he is treating you with Christ-like love, but *in everything!* The Bible does not condition your subjection on his love, even as it did not condition his love on your subjection. You must answer to God for your own actions, and no excuse for disobeying his Word will be accepted.

[1]Titus 2:4.  [2]Titus 2:5, KJV.  [3]Ephesians 5:22, 24; Colossians 3:18, Titus 2:5, 1 Peter 3:1, 5.  [4]Ephesians 5:22, TLB.  [5]Ephesians 5:24, TLB.

"But my husband never considers my feelings. I've got to stand up for my rights." Aren't you disputing the Word and wisdom of your omniscient God? Do you think for a moment that he did not know about your circumstances when he wrote his Word? He says that you are to be in submission to your husband in *everything*. He must have known that this would be best for you, or he would never have asked it of you. Give your will to him; tell him that you are willing to be the submissive partner. Obedience to this command glorifies God richly.

"But my husband is a jellyfish. He makes Charlie Brown look like the Rock of Gibraltar. How can I submit to him and lean on him?" Try it! Try submitting to him as unto the Lord, in everything. Just obey the Word and entrust the consequences to the Lord! Defer to your husband's judgment when he really ought to make the decision. Express some confidence in his abilities instead of running him down, ridiculing him, belittling him, or comparing him with other men. Tell him that you think he's the greatest, and that you thank God for having him to lean on. Watch God use your attitude to make a man out of him, the man God wants him to be.

Just as God planned for a husband's love to meet his wife's needs, so he planned for the wife's submission to meet her husband's needs. While a woman's God-given nature is to be dependent, a man senses an inner urge to take charge. No matter what he says or how he acts, he deeply resents any tactic his wife may use to dominate or manipulate him. Furthermore, a leader must have respect and recognition, and that is exactly what God wants the wife to provide. "The wife must see to it that she deeply respects her husband."[6] God made the husband to lead; the wife must let him lead, treating him as a leader should be treated.

Making a living is not easy in our competitive world. The husband often faces frustrations, discouragements, and setbacks. Some

[6]Ephesians 5:33, TLB.

people take advantage of him, cheat him, and deceive him. Others criticize or censure him. He needs someone to encourage him, to appreciate him, to believe in him, and to respect him — and that is why God gave him a wife! He will be able to bear a great deal more hardship in the workaday world if he knows that he has a wife at home who admires him, trusts him, and stands by him, whatever happens. If he gets the same sort of treatment at home that he gets in the working world, he will be tempted to try some form of escape which will lead to unhappiness for all concerned. But the thought of a smile coupled with a little admiration and encouragement will draw him to his home like a magnet.

Some may be thinking, "This submission business is all right if your husband is a Christian, but mine isn't." The central passage of Scripture on this subject is First Peter 3. It was written for all wives, but there is a special instruction to those with unsaved husbands: "Likewise, ye wives, be in subjection to your own husbands."[7] All Christian wives are to be in subjection, but read on: ". . . that, if any obey not the word (that is, if any have unbelieving husbands), they also may without a word be won by the behavior of the wives." The second occurrence of the term "word" in the verse has no definite article preceding it in the Greek text. It refers not to the Word of God, as the first occurrence, but to any word, like a nagging sermon! This is a most amazing disclosure. God says that the *subjection* of the wife is the key to winning an unbelieving husband to Christ. She doesn't have to harp about attending church. She doesn't have to preach at her husband. She doesn't have to read the Bible to him. She is simply asked to submit to him — graciously, gladly, lovingly, and tenderly. God uses this attitude, this behavior, to win her husband to Jesus Christ.

After I shared this concept with a morning Bible class I had been teaching, I noticed that one of the faithful ladies was missing for

---

[7] 1 Peter 3:1, KJV.

several succeeding weeks. Upon inquiring, I learned that her husband had been upset over her multiplied Christian activities, preferring that she stay home and tend to her household duties. After hearing what the Scriptures taught about this, she had decided to submit to him even though it involved the sacrifice of a beneficial spiritual activity which she thoroughly enjoyed. It was not long until her husband, who had previously shown little interest in the things of the Lord, trusted Christ as his Savior and began attending church with his wife to hear the Word of God for himself. He also permitted her to return to the Bible class. The consequences of conforming to God's will are always to our advantage!

"But what if my husband asks me to do something contrary to the Word of God?" This is the only exception I can find to the "everything" of Ephesians 5:24. It was Peter who commanded Christian wives to submit to their unsaved husbands. Peter also told us to obey every law of government.[8] Yet when Peter himself was rebuked by the high priest for preaching Christ, he answered, "We must obey God rather than men!"[9]

This same idea is found in Paul's Letter to the Colossians. "Wives, submit yourselves unto your own husbands, as it is fit in the Lord."[10] The basic intent here seems to be that wives are to subject themselves to their husbands because this is proper for a woman who knows the Lord. But the wording may also imply that this subjection applies only to those areas which the Lord considers proper or fitting. If subjection to the husband is really subjection to the Lord, as Ephesians 5:22 states, then it is obviously governed by the higher authority of the Lord's Word. For example, if a husband asks his Christian wife to participate in a wife-swapping party, she would have to refuse, since this activity would clearly contradict God's revealed will. Subjection in dishonorable matters eventually

[8]1 Peter 2:13, TLB.    [9]Acts 5:29, TLB.    [10]Colossians 3:18, KJV.

causes an unsaved husband to despise his Christian wife, thus driving him even farther from Christ.

How about church attendance? The Bible commands believers to assemble together,[11] but it does not say how often. A Christian wife may properly desire to be at church whenever the doors are open, but because she is in subjection to her husband she will go only when he allows her to go, graciously submitting to him when he denies her that privilege. She will let him know that she is genuinely pleased to do what makes him happy. Then she will find the strength to sustain this gracious attitude through her own personal fellowship with Christ. He in turn will reward her with additional wisdom for every new situation that arises.[12]

Viewed in the light of God's Word, subjection is not a forced slavery to which a wife must make herself conform. It is not a loss of individuality or personality. True biblical subjection is a woman's creative and challenging pleasure of discovering how she can show her husband that she respects him, admires him, and depends on him. That requires the death of all pride and the destruction of all selfish motives. It means that the wife will become more interested in the husband's needs than in her own. It means that she will stop asking, "How far must I go in my subjection to my husband?" and will instead begin to ask, "How far can I go without disobeying my Lord?" This may require a complete change of the wife's attitude toward her husband, but God will help her if she asks him. Her new prayer will be, "Lord, give me a simple and unselfish desire to be led by my husband as I am led by you, and thereby bring glory to your name."

Now let's look at a few other things which God wants every Christian wife to know, whether her husband is a believer or not. "Don't be concerned about the outward beauty that depends on jewelry, or beautiful clothes, or hair arrangement. Be beautiful in-

---

[11]Hebrews 10:25.    [12]James 1:5.

side, in your hearts, with the lasting charm of a gentle and quiet spirit which is so precious to God."[13] From the Greek word translated "outward beauty" we get our English word "cosmetic," denoting a beautifying agent. The Word of God tells Christian women how to be beautiful. If they will take this advice they will save themselves considerable expense! Peter says that beauty is not primarily a matter of external things, such as hair style, jewelry, and clothing, but instead originates in the heart. He is not saying that a Christian woman ought to be slovenly or careless about her appearance, but that real beauty is something deeper than either her skin or the threads that cover her skin!

Women need to learn this. Some seem to think that God gives them husbands to buy them everything their hearts desire. They drive their husbands to make more money so they can buy more clothing and jewelry and have their hair done more often, thereby impressing people with their beauty and social status! They use their husbands to satisfy their own pride of appearance and lust for material things. A woman like this usually destroys her husband or drives him to someone who loves him for himself.

Something that never wears out or goes out of style is ". . . a meek and quiet spirit, which is in the sight of God of great price." "Meek" means gentle, considerate, willing to surrender one's personal rights. "Quiet" means peaceful, restful, undisturbed. A meek and quiet spirit is a precious and beautiful thing in God's eyes, a thing of supreme value. But if my conversations with Christian husbands reflect the prevailing state of affairs, this trait is glaringly absent among women generally — even Christian women.

We often find instead moodiness, irritability, nagging, grumbling, and complaining — hardly commendable traits in a Christian woman! "But," some will protest, "you said in the preceding chapter that it is our physical makeup that causes us to be emotionally weak and

[13]1 Peter 3:3, 4, TLB.

moody." True, but not *all* moodiness can be attributed to body chemistry. In fact, much of it may stem from a refusal to get down off the throne of one's life and let Jesus Christ take control. This kind of refusal is sin. Irritability is one of the most common complaints of husbands and wives against each other, and it usually results from one partner interfering with the pleasure, comfort, convenience, or well-being of the other partner. Irritability is really nothing more than our sin nature having its own way. That sin nature needs to be dethroned and defeated!

This fact does not give a husband the right to be unloving or unkind when his wife is in a bad mood. She still needs words of sympathy and understanding rather than angry retorts like "Snap out of it" or "Stop acting so childishly." But neither can a wife blame her bad disposition on her husband. She must accept the responsibility for it personally before the Lord. She must call it what it is — sin. Then she must confess it to God and claim his power and grace to overcome it. The Lord Jesus Christ will then produce in her his own graciousness and sweetness.

Admittedly, a woman's life can be difficult. The burden of keeping up a home and caring for the children can easily become a monotonous routine. She goes through the motions, but feels as though she is not contributing anything significant to life. The constant confinement of four walls and the incessant backdrop of childish chatter threaten to drive her to distraction. But if she allows that attitude to linger it will cast a dismal gloom over the whole household, and everyone in it will suffer. A cheerful atmosphere in the home depends largely on the wife. If she accepts her responsibility to create a congenial atmosphere and yields herself to the indwelling Spirit of God, he will produce in her his fruit of joy; life will become an exciting challenge rather than an exasperating chore. Sometimes women get involved in so many outside activities they lose sight of the biblical priorities. Their first responsibility is to make their husbands and their homes happy — and this takes serious thought, careful planning, and selfless attention. The dividends are rich, however, and the personal satisfactions and rewards are well worth the effort.

King Lemuel describes an amazing woman in the last chapter of Proverbs. It would profit every Christian wife to read this chapter often. She is a talented woman. In fact, she even helps with the income.[14] It is not wrong for a wife to pursue a career if it does not interfere with her domestic responsibilities. Judging from all that she does for her family, the ideal woman of Proverbs 31 is an industrious, self-disciplined woman who schedules her time carefully. Nothing is too much trouble for her. She even rises before daybreak to prepare breakfast for her family.[15] One word is probably more important than any other in the passage. It is the word that describes her sustaining attitude: "She worketh *willingly* with her hands."[16] The literal meaning is "with pleasure." Her deepest joy and satisfaction is found in making her family happy. You see, the Lord is interested not only in what we do, but also in how we do it. Our attitude matters to him. When a Christian wife is yielded to Christ she will be able to accept her God-given role joyfully, and her husband's heart will cry "Amen" when he reads the words, "The man who finds a wife finds a good thing; she is a blessing to him from the Lord!"[17]

A word of caution must be given to the husbands, too. It is so easy to talk about the faults of our mates instead of seeking God's grace to improve our own shortcomings. This chapter was not written for husbands to hold over their wives. It was written so that the Holy Spirit can enlighten Christian wives about their biblical duties. Let each of us examine our own lives in the light of the Word; the Holy Spirit will perform his work in your mate in his own divine way!

[14]Proverbs 31:16.  [15]Proverbs 31:15.  [16]Proverbs 31:13, KJV.  [17]Proverbs 18:22, TLB.

# CHAPTER TEN

# SPEAKING THE TRUTH IN LOVE

One of the most common problem areas in troubled marriages is a lack of communication. This situation is partly a product of our society, for many children grow up in homes where little constructive communication ever takes place. Family togetherness has degenerated to a joint television viewing; anyone who dares to say anything is told to keep quiet because the others cannot hear! The latest trend is for each family member to have his own TV, so that he can watch what he wants without distractions or interruptions. All inter-family communication is thus destroyed.

Another factor which contributes to the absence of family communication is our tendency to prevent our children from expressing their true feelings. We usually consider it more important to act and speak in a socially acceptable manner than to express our actual thoughts. Thus, after a child has made an especially embarrassing remark we may expect to hear his mother reply, "Junior, don't ever say that again! What will people think?" We should certainly consider the feelings of others, but our undue concern about other people's opinions encourages Junior to keep his innermost thoughts and feelings to himself, thereby avoiding the pain of being misunderstood and rejected. He thus learns to suppress communication.

Soon he enters the competitive world of school, and later of employment. Few people care about his thoughts or feelings; his *performance* is all that counts. He is accepted by his superiors only as long as he conforms to certain standards and produces a specific quality of work. His job security might be threatened if people could see inside and discover what he really thinks. So he learns to conceal what is there, to present a self-image which impresses people, one which hides his faults and weaknesses. Behind his façade he feels as impersonal as a computer card. He wants to be accepted as he is, but no one will do it, for no one has found out who he really is.

Then the inevitable happens — he finds himself attracted to a person of the opposite sex. He begins to open up, to share his inner feelings. His companion does the same, and it becomes a thrilling experience. At last they have each found someone who really understands, who accepts the other party for what he actually is. They find that they have much in common, that they were "made for each other." When the marrying pastor asks if they are able to communicate with each other, they confidently assert that this is one of their greatest assets.

As the marriage wears on, however, they have less and less to talk about. What they once thought was a deep understanding of each other turns out to have been merely the first exciting attempt to explore the mystery of each other's personality. But now the novelty is gone. As the pressures of the marital routine mount, communicating becomes an unpleasant experience. Tensions increase, misunderstandings occur, unkind words are spoken, and feelings are hurt. The disenchantment becomes unbearable. The more each expresses his opinion the more unpleasant the atmosphere becomes, until they revert to concealing their inner thoughts. Instead of growing in their knowledge and understanding of each other, with more and more of their lives shared in the oneness which God planned for them, they drift farther and farther apart.

So the complaints come: "He never talks to me anymore." "He won't tell me anything about his work." "I don't know what she really thinks." "She won't stop running off at the mouth long enough to hear my side of it." On and on they go. Did you know that the Bible has a great deal to say about communications problems?

First of all, it explains why we let communications break down.

Inside each of us is an old, sinful nature. In addition to being weak and frail, it is unbelievably selfish and corrupt. "The heart is the most deceitful thing there is, and desperately wicked. No one can really know how bad it is!"[1] It is embarrassing to expose our deceitful hearts, so we wear a mask of respectability rather than reveal our true natures. Jesus said that men love darkness rather than light because their deeds are evil.[2] We prefer to keep our innermost thoughts and motives concealed in the darkness of our hearts, lest they be illuminated for all to see! Since the thoughts of our hearts have a tendency to come out of our mouths,[3] we often guard our mouths carefully. We avoid getting too close to anyone, lest we be tempted to divulge our weaknesses, and people see us as we really are!

This is not to suggest that we tell our mates all our past sins. It is possible that God may want us to do this, but it might also be the most ruthless thing we could ever do to them. We should, however, stop putting on airs while our hearts are corrupted with lust, pride, hatred, and jealousy or riddled with doubts and anxieties.

The greatest thing that could ever happen to some marriages would be for the high and mighty husband or the holier-than-thou wife to step down off his pedestal of self-righteousness and confess his weakness and need. Such humility could dissolve growing resentments, rekindle waning love, and reestablish broken lines of communication. To pretend to be something which we are not is the essence of hypocrisy, and no group ever drew a more scathing denunciation from the lips of the Lord Jesus than the hypocrites.[4]

Again, I am not suggesting that we blurt out everything that comes into our minds. That becomes an offense to others, and God is not honored in this either. "Give no offense, neither to the Jews, nor to the Greeks, nor to the church of God."[5] The first step toward letting Christ transform our lives is to admit that we are not what

[1] Jeremiah 17:9, TLB.  [2] John 3:19.  [3] Matthew 12:34.  [4] cf. Matthew 23.
[5] 1 Corinthians 10:32, KJV.

we should be, that we need to be changed. There are few situations in life more miserable than being married to an unbending, self-sufficient individual, someone who thinks his opinions are infallible and his actions impeccable.

One of the most frustrating counseling situations I have ever faced involved just such a person. Fred suffered an acute hearing deficiency which he had never fully accepted or learned to live with. It made him excessively intolerant and unreasonable with his wife and children. What he said was law; it was never to be doubted or questioned. He made rash decisions without knowing all the facts and tolerated no appeal. He could do no wrong in his own eyes, and would not admit to being at fault about anything. Twenty-five years of his domineering dogmatism and stubbornness had totally alienated his grown children from him and had made his wife the most bitter person I ever met. The only communication which took place between them was shouting and screaming, some of which I heard during a visit to their home.

In a private session I tactfully explained to Fred that some of the conflicts in his life might have been intensified by his personal attitudes. He rose from his chair and paced the floor of my study restlessly. "It is possible, I suppose," he finally observed, "but I never really thought about it that way." His subsequent actions revealed that he decided never to think about it that way again. A simple acknowledgment of some part of the blame might have begun to melt away the resentment which the years had built, thereby initiating the healing process that was so desperately needed. But his pride would not let him step down. He chose to seal the doom of his marriage rather than acknowledge any fault. Meaningful communication was cut off at its source.

The Bible hints at another reason we refuse to communicate: we fear our spouse's reaction. Some people simply fall to pieces when they are told of their shortcomings. There may be a volcanic out-burst, an angry tirade, gushing tears, or a long period of sullen silence. Once we learn what evokes this kind of response in our mates, we fear to produce this type of situation again. We see no point in subjecting ourselves to unnecessary anguish, so we draw into a silent shell of self-protection. The next time we ask why our spouses will not talk to us, let us first ask ourselves how we reacted to previous disclosures! We may discover that the blame lies with us.

The biblical corrective for this kind of a communications crisis is, "Stop being mean, bad-tempered and angry. Quarreling, harsh words, and dislike of others should have no place in your lives. In-stead, be kind to each other, tenderhearted, forgiving one another, just as God has forgiven you because you belong to Christ."[6] When your mate opens his heart and you are tempted to respond with condemnation, pray before you open your mouth! "Lord, keep me from anger; keep me from saying anything unkind. Help me to lis-ten carefully and sympathetically to my mate, to try to understand his feelings, to see this matter from his point of view." Then com-municate intelligently and meaningfully, unimpaired by emotional outbursts.

Make it a rule never to raise your voice. Loud voices are un-pleasant, and few people enjoy unpleasantness. Loud, bitter, angry, sarcastic words will only drive your mate deeper into his shell. Listen to King Solomon: "A soft answer turns away wrath, but harsh words cause quarrels."[7] Memorize this verse. "Soft" refers not only to the volume level, but also to the *empathy* level. Kind and gentle words pour cold water on the burning coals of a stirred-up spirit. Harsh words only add fuel to the fire. How should you react when your mate opens his heart? With kindness, calmness, graciousness, and gentleness. That keeps the lines of communication open.

Still another obstacle to sharing may be fear that our mates will

[6]Ephesians 4:31, 32, TLB.    [7]Proverbs 15:1, TLB.

use the information against us at some future time. When differences of opinion occur, some people love to drag skeletons out of closets and rehash old weaknesses, mistakes, and failures. We really cannot expect our mates to unburden their souls to us if they know they are going to hear a replay next month or next year. A person who brings up old issues is more interested in being right and winning arguments than in building an intimate personal relationship with his marriage partner.

The words "forgiving one another, just as God has forgiven you because you belong to Christ"[8] are also pertinent to this problem. Some people protest, "But I *have* forgiven. It's just that I can't forget." How does God forgive? "I will forgive and forget their sins."[9] "He has removed our sins as far away from us as the east is from the west."[10] If our mates could trust us never to use their confidential disclosures as a future arsenal against them, they would be more open with us. There is only one way to gain this trust: by asking God to help us forgive and forget. He may not exterminate the memory from our minds, but he will extract the sting from it, thereby removing any reason for ever mentioning it again!

A beautifully happy marriage is only possible when each partner knows how the other feels about most of the situations and issues that face them both. This kind of empathy demands open lines of communication. We sometimes develop the erroneous idea that the best alternative to an angry argument is complete silence. We feel that we deserve a special reward if we bite our tongues in stony silence while our mates rant and rave. But this kind of silence buys us a ticket to the hospital with any of several stress-related diseases, and it further infuriates our mates as well. There is another alternative to angry argument. It is sharing in love what is on our hearts! The Bible reveals not only the roadblocks to communication, but the pathways to communication as well! One short phrase in Ephesians

[8]Ephesians 4:32, TLB.   [9]Jeremiah 31:34, TLB.   [10]Psalm 103:12, TLB.

4:15 holds the key to effective communication in the home: "speaking the truth in love."

The first principle is to be honest: "speaking the *truth*." A satisfying marriage relationship will involve openness and honesty about fears, desires, motivations, sex, money, weaknesses, mistakes, resentments, and misunderstandings. Many marital problems could be resolved if husbands and wives were only honest with each other. Are you having problems that you have kept from your mate in order to spare him worry? If so, you are actually shutting him out of your life by implying that he is not emotionally strong enough or spiritually mature enough to help you resolve your problems. That is a backhanded insult that will only pull you farther apart.

Do you have needs which your mate could be fulfilling, but is not? You have been too proud or too ashamed to admit it, so you have tried to be a martyr and keep it to yourself. Soon inner tensions and resentments will build to the point of a major crisis that needs professional counsel. That is a high price to pay for a little dishonesty.

The second principle of effective communication is to be loving, "speaking the truth *in love*." The truth can sometimes be cruel. That is why God says it must be spoken *in love*. This involves a genuine consideration for the other person. Some brutal things have been told in the name of honesty when the real reason was to get out from under the pangs of a guilty conscience. The great goal in marriage is complete openness and total intimacy of soul and spirit. This, however, does not happen overnight. It sometimes takes years to accomplish, and some couples never fully arrive. But God wants us to keep growing, each day exposing a little more of our souls to each other in Christian love and courtesy.

Love also helps us choose the right time to share bad news or to introduce some difficult subject. "Timely advice is as lovely as golden apples in a silver basket."[11] "How wonderful it is to be able to say the right thing at the right time!"[12] Both of these verses refer to appropriate words spoken at the right time. It is usually a good policy to wait until after supper to discuss unpleasant or controversial matters. Sometimes it is best to wait until morning, especially if our mates have had a particularly trying day.

If the issue we wish to discuss is some fault in our spouses, love will cause us to talk to the Lord first. He may show us that the problem is really their reaction to some poor trait in *us* — something which *we* need to deal with first. Then, if the Lord gives us liberty to bring it up, love will help us preface our remarks with some word of commendation or appreciation, and we will present our thoughts pleasantly, constructively, and positively. We will encourage rather than injure our mates. "Kind words are like honey — enjoyable and healthful."[13]

We really cannot even begin to talk about someone else's faults without heeding this advice of the Apostle Paul: "Dear brothers, if a Christian is overcome by some sin, you who are godly should gently and humbly help him back onto the right path, remembering that next time it might be one of you who is in the wrong."[14] It is so easy to sound superior when we talk to others about their shortcomings. It makes us appear a little holier than they! But God says that we are to approach others with meekness, since we are subject to the same weaknesses that they are. True meekness is the fruit of the Spirit's control in our lives; we therefore cannot properly discuss the faults of our mates unless we ourselves are filled with the Spirit. When he is in control we will sound neither harsh nor unkind, nor will we imply for a moment that we are faultless ourselves.

Love will likewise keep us from using passion-arousing generalizations like "always" or "never." "You never listen to me." "You

11Proverbs 25:11, TLB.    12Proverbs 15:23, TLB.    13Proverbs 16:24, TLB.
14Galatians 6:1, TLB.

always interrupt me." Such generalizations are seldom true. Love will also keep us from arguing in front of others, especially the children, and from talking about the frailities of our mates to others. "Love shall *cover* the multitude of sins."[15]

Love will help us learn when to stop talking as well. Solomon said there is a time to speak and a time to be silent.[16] Not all talking is meaningful communication. Our mates may want to unveil their souls and share something very important with us if only we will stop talking long enough to let them. Love will also keep us from forcing our mates to share what they do not want to share at the moment. Love always considers the other person. It is the spiritual medicine powerful enough to cure almost all of the communication ills in any Christian home. "Speak the truth in love."

Communication is the means by which we learn to know and understand our mates. God, however, already understands our mates; he created them. Let us ask him to open our channels of interpersonal communication and give us the same understanding that he has, that our marriage relationship may grow increasingly precious every day.

[15]1 Peter 4:8, KJV.    [16]Ecclesiastes 3:7.

# CHAPTER ELEVEN

# SOLVING MARITAL CONFLICTS

No matter how well we are communicating with our marriage partners, there are bound to be some areas of disagreement. I have heard some couples claim that they never had a difference of opinion during all their married life. What a drab and colorless existence they must have had! The couple either possessed very little personal individuality or else were afraid to express their true inner feelings. It is hard to believe that God ever made two people so alike in every way that their opinions coincided in everything!

Disagreements will come. Any of several causes can produce them. The first cause could easily be the rude discovery that our mates do not possess all the glowing qualities we visualized in them before the ceremony! Since we want to see desirable traits acquired and distasteful ones eliminated, we mentally enroll our mates in our school of marital reform! Then we proceed with the monumental task of remaking them into ideal mates.

The wife's favorite teaching method seems to be nagging, assisted by occasional ridicule, and, if necessary, by a periodic outburst of tears. The husband's favorite teaching method seems to be the dig, that is, the cutting comment or sarcastic remark. He may also use an occasional angry lecture, interspersed with long periods of withdrawal and silence. Two sinful self-wills, each of which is torn between love of self and love of mate, are now interacting with each other and testing each other's right to self-determination, with each seeking supremacy in the relationship. The result is conflict.

At the heart of every conflict is self. Most people blame their conflicts on their circumstances: the unacceptable job, the small house, the fussy children, the poor neighborhood, the lack of money, the interfering in-laws. But the true problem is that the human ego wants unrestrained freedom to do as it pleases, expecting at the same time the unqualified approval of its mate. In other words, it wants to be the sun around which its mate orbits as a devoted planet. If two such stars would vie for centrality in the same solar system, the results would be chaotic — but that is exactly what has happened in many marriages!

Sometimes young people are in a hurry to get married, often to escape an unpleasant situation at home. The real problem is not usually their home or their parents, however. It is their own sinful egos, and they invariably take them along with them when they get married! This ego begins to interact with another selfish ego, and the previous home problems are eclipsed by the new marital ones! First God wants us to learn how to deal with our old sin natures. Then we will be ready to interact happily with a partner in marriage.

When meaningful communications have broken down in a marriage, arguments may erupt over the most trivial things, sometimes becoming so frequent and so heated that the couple begins to feel that they are incompatible. I seriously doubt that there is any such thing as incompatibility in God's sight — just two wills that need to be conquered by Jesus Christ. When he becomes the center of the marriage, with each partner living for his glory, harmony and happiness will reign supreme.

Suppose the conflicts do exist, however, and the couple is willing to make the spiritual adjustments that need to be made. How, then, do we resolve the dissension in our marriages? We need to realize, first of all, that an argument need not always be a destructive force. It could be the very thing needed to open the channels of communication and expose the festering sores of the soul that have been widening the gap between us. There may be some changes that need to be made, but neither the nagging nor the cutting comments are making them. They only tighten the tension and drive us farther apart. A good, lively discussion may be the only thing that will get our true feelings into the open. If so, then we need to get to it, to get started with the argument. But we must set some ground rules before we begin. Here are some suggested guidelines for a profitable argument.

First, we must establish as our goal a deeper understanding of each other. If we can accomplish this, we will ultimately thank God for the disagreement. The goal of the argument is *not to decide a winner and a loser.* Nor is it to bring about changes in our mates. It is to gain fresh insight into how our mates think about the issues that affect us. It might be a good policy for each partner to restate the other's point of view to his satisfaction. That will guarantee the accomplishment of this goal, at least to some degree.

Second, we must ask God to help us control our emotions. We often say things under emotional stress that we do not mean, things that hurt and cut and destroy. These things are not soon forgotten. The fruit of the Spirit is self-control, and we need to let him manifest his calmness and control even in the face of unjust accusations or serious provocations. This is not to say that emotions should be excluded. We would probably never reveal how we felt in our hearts if emotions were not present. But though it is legitimate for our emotions to be present, they must be guarded closely by the indwelling Holy Spirit. One wife told me that whenever their discussions begin to heat up, her husband says, "Let's pray about this," and he begins to pray, out loud. It has a tremendously tranquilizing effect on their marriage!

Third, we must attack the problem itself — not the personalities or the motives. It is easy to become overly critical in any argument, and to make inaccurate character judgments of our opponent or to falsely accuse him of evil motives. When a wife fails to clean the house or a husband postpones some chore, the impatient mate may level an accusation like, "You're just plain lazy." That may not be the problem at all, and such an accusation could cause a great deal of unhappiness for a long time to come. "You did that just to get back at me," is a favorite when your mate hurts you in some way. But who made you a mind reader or gave you the ability to discern motives? The Apostle Paul made an astute observation about people who judge others. "Therefore, thou art inexcusable, O man, whosoever thou art that judgest; for wherein thou judgest another, thou condemnest thyself; for thou that judgest doest the same things."[1] We have a tendency to project our own motives to others; our angry accusations against our mates thus often reveal more about our own hearts than of theirs. Christ said that we will be judged by the same standard we applied to them, "For with what judgment ye judge, ye shall be judged."[2]

Fourth, we must remember that angry attacks against us are sometimes provoked by exasperating incidents totally unrelated to us. Often when husbands or wives are irritable, their mates just happen to be the most convenient target for their angry outbursts. For instance, the pressure of the house and the children may have been building up in a wife all day long. She is tense and on edge when her husband comes in the door, happy as a lark. He hangs up his coat as a thoughtful husband should, but forgets to close the closet door — and she blows her top! A husband filled with God's love and understanding realizes that there is something more behind this than a closet door, and he responds tenderly and gently. Maybe the husband comes home acting like an angry bear. He is short with the children and critical of the dinner. A Spirit-filled wife understands that his actions are probably the result of pressure at work and not of hostility toward his family. If we would listen to our mates calmly and patiently instead of reacting indignantly

[1]Romans 2:1, KJV.    [2]Matthew 7:2, KJV.

at the first provocation, the real problem would soon emerge. Then, instead of an irate retort, we could offer sympathetic understanding, thus averting the trauma of an argument.

Finally, we need to learn when and how to bring an argument to a conclusion. Some fights never end; they just go on for years! Others seem to die without coming to a conclusion, thus deepening the underlying resentment. "Let's just forget about it" usually means, "If we discuss this much longer, I may have to give in!" If we are wrong, we should admit it. If we need time to think about it, we should say so. "I'm beginning to see your point, but I need some time to think it over." Then do just that — think it over before the Lord.

Now the problems are out in the open. We have communicated with each other and therefore share a little deeper understanding. Now where do we go? How do we solve the conflicts? There are several biblical principles that should help us.

First, we should concentrate our attention on our *own* faults, thinking first of those areas in which we can improve *ourselves*. The temptation when conflicts arise is to sulk over the wrongs committed against us, rehearsing all the old offenses and injustices we have suffered through the years. Then we begin building our case for the next confrontation! Forget it! Turn your mind to *your* part of the blame, however small it may be. Our own self-will and pride are invariably responsible for part of the conflict. It may have been the little demands we made of our mates for our own convenience. It may have been the indifference we showed toward our mates' needs. It may have been the coolness we expressed because our feelings were hurt. All of this is selfish pride, and all of it helped intensify the conflict. Whenever there is a conflict pride is the cause,[3] and each of us is usually guilty of some of that pride. We need to admit it.

[3]Proverbs 13:10.

It's so easy to let our minds drift to our spouses' part of the blame. We are tempted to think that we acted as we did because of what our mates said or did. We think *they* are really the guilty ones. But this is a ploy of Satan. He wants us to think about our mate's blame rather than our own in order to promote dissension. Jesus called this hypocrisy. "Hypocrite! First get rid of the board. Then you can see to help your brother."[4] Let us ask God to help us acknowledge our own part of the blame. We must be ruthless with ourselves. It is so easy to be severe with others and lenient with ourselves. But this is egotism. True humility is tolerant of others and exacting with self. Once we acknowledge our sin of pride, God bestows both forgiveness and renewed marital harmony.

Now that we have acknowledged our part of the blame and received God's gracious forgiveness, we can ask him to give us victory over our sinful self-wills, so that we relinquish our craving to have everything our own way. We must ask him to help us change what needs to be changed in our lives. When we are in the middle of a marital crisis we usually feel that our problems would be solved if only our mates would change their ways. It seldom occurs to us that *we* need the changing! By God's grace we can become new mates. We never really change others for the better by carping, criticizing, and complaining. We only deepen the wedge that lies between us. We must give our attention to the one thing that we *can* change by God's grace and power — *ourselves!* God does not expect us to improve our mates; he expects us to provide for their needs. When we improve ourselves, our marriages will also begin to improve.

When our husbands or wives realize that we have stopped badgering them and have instead made significant changes in our own lives, they will begin to respond in kind. It will take terribly cold and calloused hearts on their part to keep them from making some

[4]Matthew 7:5, TLB.

worthwhile changes of their own. What a gratifying reward for our unselfish attitude!

Having dealt decisively with our own shortcomings, we are now ready to move on to the next step. The second biblical principle for solving conflicts is to forgive completely our mates' faults. It is hard to forgive when our mates have not apologized. But look at it this way. If we have really acknowledged our part of the blame, we will have to admit that the offenses they committed against us may have been, at least in part, a result of the way we treated them. We have no choice but to forgive, even if they have not admitted their wrong. Eventually we are going to have to apologize for our part of the blame if we want a sweet spirit of harmony restored, and we will not be able to apologize in the proper way if we continue to harbor hard feelings. The only way to rid ourselves of those hard feelings is to forgive our mates fully for every offense that they have committed against us. There is no indication that the person who was wronging Peter ever apologized for it, yet Christ told him to forgive as many as 490 times.[5] He was teaching that there is actually no end to forgiveness.

"But the hurt is too deep. I can't forgive." That is an interesting comment. Listen to Christ again: "Your heavenly Father will forgive you if you forgive those who sin against you; but if *you* refuse to forgive *them,* he will not forgive *you.*"[6] At first sight this would seem to teach that our own forgiveness is based on our forgiveness of others, instead of on God's grace in Christ. However, this would contradict Christ's other teachings. I believe he is saying, instead, that if we refuse to forgive the person who has wronged us, God knows that the confession of our own sins to him has been less than genuine, and that we have not really received the forgiveness which he has made available to us. When a person has admitted the vileness of his own sin and has experienced the blessing of God's forgiveness, he cannot help but respond with forgiveness toward others. If we refuse, we admit that we have really not known what it means to be forgiven by God. No honest person can receive God's forgiveness himself but refuse to forgive another.

It is impossible to overestimate the importance of forgiveness. When we grant forgiveness, resentment and bitterness disappear and our harsh and intolerant attitudes are replaced with genuine love and concern for our mates.

Now we are ready for the final step. We have admitted to ourselves our own guilt and have forgiven our mates for their share of the blame. Now we must openly and frankly apologize to them for our part of the blame. It is a mistake to try to apologize before we have acknowledged our own guilt and forgiven our mates for theirs. Our apology will be far less than what God wants it to be. It will come out all wrong, and may even do more harm than good. "I was wrong, but you were, too." "I'm sorry I did that, but it wasn't all my fault." "I'm sorry I said that, but what could I think after what you did?" "I'm sorry *if* I did anything to offend you." None of these statements really admits to anything. They are not true apologies and really won't fool anybody — least of all our mates!

Only after our hearts have been set right before the Lord can we offer a genuine apology. "Honey, I'm sorry I . . . (and we list the specific things we did or said to offend, or the exact attitude that has contributed to the conflict) — *period!* No "ifs," "ands," or "buts." The words "Honey, I'm sorry" spoken from a broken and contrite heart are the sweetest sound on earth, and they will minister healing to our marriages. This is what James meant when he wrote, "Admit your faults to one another and pray for each other so that you may be healed."[7] Though he was referring primarily to physical healing, the same truth can be applied to the mending of marital

James 5:16, TLB.

relationships. Open and sincere admission of guilt is a powerful healing force.

Why is it so hard for some people to apologize? Possibly they tried apologizing once or twice but were rejected. Now they are afraid to try again. But the reason for their rejection may have been their own improper attitude when they offered the apology. Some men think that admitting guilt is a sign of weakness. Actually, however, it is a sign of spiritual and emotional strength — a mark of a healthy, well-balanced personality. Some people are afraid that they will lose face with the ones they love if they admit their faults. But the very opposite is true; by being honest about themselves, they will actually gain *more* respect than they ever had before. Some insist that it would be hypocritical to apologize, since they will probably do the same thing again. But God says that we are to confess our faults to each other. Refusal is disobedience to him. We must deal with the issue at hand as he directs, trusting him to help us in future situations.

Jesus taught that we must be reconciled with others before we can truly worship God. "If you are standing before the altar in the Temple, offering a sacrifice to God, and suddenly remember that a friend has something against you, leave your sacrifice there beside the altar and go and apologize and be reconciled to him, and then come and offer your sacrifice to God."[8] If someone has something against us, it is probably because we have offended him. It is our responsibility to go to him, admit our fault, and be reconciled to him. Our worship will be less than it should be until we do. "But isn't he supposed to forgive me even if I refuse to apologize?" Yes, he is. But each person must nevertheless answer to God for himself. We must do what God wants *us* to do, leaving the failures of others in the hands of God.

The question "Who started it?" or "Who ought to make the first

[8]Matthew 5:23, 24, TLB.

move?" is irrelevant. It makes no difference who started it. We ought to take the initiative in confession regardless of the situation. Even if we have been deeply hurt, to admit our part of the blame in unselfish and forgiving love will make it easier for our mates to admit theirs. No matter how minor our fault is, we ought to focus our attention on that and frankly apologize for it. God will then use our selfless spirit to resolve our marital conflicts.

I shared some of these concepts with a young wife and mother named Lynn. Her husband had a job that often demanded long and unexpected hours. He felt no obligation to keep her informed when he worked late, and many lovely meals were thoroughly spoiled because of his lack of consideration. When he did come home, he would rush through his dinner, sometimes without saying a word to her, then leave home immediately to enjoy his hobby late into the night. He spent no time whatsoever with their three small children, and they barely knew him.

After our discussion Lynn agreed that, with God's help, she would concentrate on the things that needed improving in her own life, giving special attention to meeting Jack's needs. She would commit his inconsiderateness to the Lord in faith. Shortly afterward I learned that Jack's job would take them nearly five hundred miles away. About a year later I received this encouraging letter from Lynn:

*Dear Dr. Strauss,*

*I just wanted to write and thank you for your advice. It really worked. Our marriage and our personal relationship have completely changed. I began to forget about myself and the things I felt I deserved and needed, and tried to think about Jack and his needs. At first it was most difficult, but as I yielded myself to the Lord, it became easier and easier each day. Soon I didn't even have to try — it just seemed to come automatically.*

*Then things began to change. Jack started calling me from work to tell me when he would be later for dinner than he had planned. He never did that before. He started taking time to sit down and play with the children instead of running out right after dinner. It's so much easier to talk to him now about the disagreements we have periodically. He doesn't get mad as easy as he once did. Our family is so much happier than before, and it wasn't really so hard to follow your suggestions. Thank you ever so much.*

*Sincerely,*
*Lynn*

No, it really isn't so hard to do what God asks us to in his Word! If we honestly want to see our marriages changed we will trust him to help us make the first move.

# CHAPTER TWELVE

# MONEY, MONEY, MONEY!

"Money isn't everything in life, but it's far ahead of whatever is in second place." That famous quip is wrong; money is not life's most important ingredient. Nevertheless, the significance of money should not be treated lightly. Some Christians consider it unspiritual to be interested in money; the plain truth, however, is that we cannot live without it and the Lord's work cannot continue without it. If Christian people used more of their money for evangelistic outreaches, the gospel of Jesus Christ would make a far greater impact on this needy world. For the sake of the gospel, as well as for our own sakes, we need to learn how to manage money.

Our Christian testimony depends in part on the proper management of money. The Christian who does not pay his bills is a poor testimony to the saving power of Christ. The believer whose finances are a fiasco is a poor testimony to the wisdom and guidance of God. The husband and wife who are at war over money are a poor testimony to the love and peace of the Holy Spirit. Money ranks high on every family counselor's list of problem areas in marriage. Someone has estimated that at least sixty percent of all married couples have had some degree of conflict over money. Since so much hinges on our ability to handle our finances properly, we need to learn what God's Word has to say about this subject.

The Bible never suggests that it is a sin to be rich. On the contrary, some great men of faith have been among the wealthiest people of their day — men like Job, Abraham, David, and Solomon. It was the Lord himself who gave these men their riches, for it is he who holds the reins of wealth.[1] However, while *money itself* is not sinful,

[1]Deuteronomy 8:18.

the *love of money* is the root of all kinds of evil.[2] People who set their hearts on getting more money may eventually stoop to anything to achieve their goal.

It is this love for money and the things it can buy that destroys many a marriage. The Bible says that people who determine in their hearts to accumulate wealth create a trap for themselves.[3] Their dissatisfaction with what they already have creates tension, giving rise to repeated conflicts with those around them. The trouble they get into by trying to make a fast dollar brings shame and remorse to those dearest to them.

The problem is basically a matter of heart attitude. We have all met people who lived in the barest of quarters, ate the plainest of food, and wore the simplest of clothing — yet were perfectly happy! They had learned to find happiness in the Lord and in each other, and to enjoy with thankful hearts the few things they did possess. They refused to let their minds dwell on what they did *not* have. They were thoroughly convinced that "real life and real living are not related to how rich we are."[4]

On the other hand, we have all met people who perpetually want something more. Happiness always seems to be just one more gadget away. They think they could be happy if only they had another bedroom, a larger kitchen, carpeting on the floors, a swimming pool, a boat, a cabin on the lake, a second car, a color TV, or a fur coat! But when they finally get that "one more thing," they find that they need just one *more* thing to be truly happy. Before they know it, life is gone and they have missed its true joys after all. Enjoy what God has given you! Forget what you do not have. Then you will learn the real meaning of happiness.[5]

It is certainly difficult to keep our hearts away from material things in this age of the ad man. Hucksters of fancy new trinkets are harping at us everywhere we turn, assuring us that we can

[2]1 Timothy 6:10.  [3]1 Timothy 6:9.  [4]Luke 12:15, TLB.  [5]Philippians 4:11; 1 Timothy 6:6; Hebrews 13:5.

increase our popularity, insure our social acceptance, and enter into a glorious and carefree world of ecstasy if only we will buy their products. Before long they have convinced us that their products are no longer luxuries, but necessities! We simply must have them! And so Satan succeeds in diverting our affection from "things above" to "things on the earth,"[6] thereby applying still another stress to our already burdened marriages.

This "must have more" attitude is labeled for what it is in the Bible — sin. The sin of covetousness is listed with such other sins as fornication, stealing, and drunkenness.[7] Paul teaches that covetousness is equivalent to idolatry,[8] a sin vigorously denounced in both the Old and New Testaments. If we want God's fullness of peace in our marriages, we will have to conquer our covetousness. "You cannot serve God and money."[9] When we get victory in this attitude of living, many of our other money problems in marriage will also be solved, since most of them are traceable to the selfish craving for material things on the part of one or both partners. Most money problems can be solved by learning to manage properly the money God has entrusted to us. In addition to telling us what our attitude toward money should be, the Bible presents certain basic principles regarding the administration of our money.

The first principle we should mention is that we are to give our government and our God their part first. We mention our government first because our taxes are usually taken out of our paychecks before we ever get them! We pay them first whether we like it or not. Christ mentioned government first, too: "Render to Caesar the things that are Caesar's, and to God the things that are God's."[10] Even though many of us gripe about paying our taxes, the Lord Jesus Christ himself sanctioned the government's right to levy them. The Apostle Paul added this inspired exhortation: "Pay your taxes, too. . . . Pay everyone whatever he ought to have: pay your taxes

[6]Colossians 3:2, KJV.    [7]1 Corinthians 6:9, 10.    [8]Colossians 3:5.    [9]Matthew 6:24b.    [10]Mark 12:17, KJV.

and import duties gladly, obey those over you, and give honor and respect to all those to whom it is due."[11]  Paul also said that we ought to provide things honest in the sight of all men.[12]  This would involve completing our tax forms as truthfully as if the Lord Jesus himself were looking over our shoulders!  As a matter of fact, he is![13]

After our government obligations are met we turn to God's part. If you've been saying, "When we get these debts paid off, we'll be able to give as we should," or "When we get our raise we'll be able to give the proper percentage," then you'll probably never give as you should. You have your values reversed. The most important thing on earth is the work of Jesus Christ, and it must be first in our lives if we want to be in step with him.  This means that his work must be first in our paychecks, too.  God should get his part before anything else is paid, even if we must sacrifice something we would like to have in order to give him his part.

Some professing Christians spend more on dog food, tobacco, recreation, or hobbies than they give to the work of the Lord.  Christ said, "For where your treasure is, there will your heart be also."[14]  He was establishing the fact that we come to love the things we pour our money into.  For example, if we spend every spare penny on our houses, then we will come to love those houses more than we love the Lord, and that is idolatry.  It is as nauseous to God as bowing down before an image of wood or stone.  If we are living to increase our assets, sinking every possible dollar into stocks and bonds, it will not be long before we will love those pieces of paper more than we love Jesus Christ and his work.

Conversely, if we give sacrificially to the Lord's work we will grow to love that work.  We will live to see souls come to Christ; we will take a keen interest in the needs of missionaries; we will participate

---

[11]Romans  13:6,  7,  TLB.     [12]Romans  12:17,  KJV.     [13]Hebrews  13:5. [14]Matthew 6:21, KJV.

in the prayer service, where the power for their ministry is generated. Where our treasure is, there will our hearts be also!

Maybe you are wondering how much you should give. This matter is entirely between you and the Lord. The Bible says a great deal about a tenth, and that may be a good place to begin. It is hard to imagine that most people in this land of affluence could not give at least that much to the Lord's work if they planned their budgets wisely. If you try giving a tenth, you will probably make an exciting discovery. You will find that the remaining nine-tenths will go farther than the whole paycheck went originally! The Lord has a way of making sacrificial stewardship enjoyable for the people who practice it with the proper attitude.[15] Of course, in this age of God's boundless grace we should never set a tenth as the *limit* of our giving. Many Christians can do much better than this. Our giving is to be proportionate to God's blessing,[16] and for some of us that would involve much more than a tenth. But the real point is to give whatever amount you prayerfully decide upon, and to give it *first*.

The second biblical principle for the administration of money is to lay aside a specified amount for savings. This will include, first of all, money to buy the things we believe God wants us to have. It is far better stewardship of the Lord's money to put it in the bank, where it earns interest, than to buy on time and *pay* interest. All of our money is the Lord's, and we are responsible for how we use every penny, not just the amount we give to his work. It is not a sin to buy on time. It is usually necessary with something as large as a house. Those who refuse to borrow money for a house usually quote Paul in their defense: "Owe no man anything." But Paul is simply saying that we should not *continue* to owe anybody money; that is, we should pay our debts. This does not prohibit buying on time. Before you buy anything on time, however, evaluate the

[15]2 Corinthians 9:6-8.     [16]1 Corinthians 16:2.

whole situation before God. "Do I really need this now, or will I be a better steward of God's money by waiting a little while and saving for it?" There are many things we can easily do without until we save enough to pay cash for them.

Our savings might also include long-range investments. I have known Christians who do not believe in saving for the future. They say that the Lord will take care of them, and that there is therefore no need to save. But the Lord may want to provide for us through wise planning and Spirit-directed investments. Paul mentions parents laying up for their children.[17] He also reminds us of our responsibility to provide properly for our own households.[18] Savings can serve as an emergency fund, provide for the children's education, or pay for a family visit to a mission field. Regular savings, wise investments, and adequate life insurance will be particularly helpful if the Lord should allow the husband to be taken away from his family. A wise steward of God's money will also be sure to prepare a will. No matter how young you may be or how little you may own, a will can save your loved ones untold heartache and loss. You might also investigate the advantages of remembering the Lord's work in your will.

Christ's parable of the talents certainly condones the policy of investing money to gain interest. "You should at least have put my money in the bank so I could have some interest."[19] The condemnation of usury in the scriptures does not prohibit earning interest on our money. The word "usury" indicates the charging of *excessive* interest rates, particularly toward those who are least able to pay.[20] It makes good sense to put the Lord's money to work, earning more money to use for his glory.

How much should we save? Again, this is between each individual and the Lord. I would think that less than ten percent of our total income for all these different facets of saving would not be of

[17]2 Corinthians 12:14.    [18]1 Timothy 5:8.    [19]Matthew 25:27, TLB.    [20]Exodus 22:25; Leviticus 25:35-37; Deuteronomy 23:19, 20.

very much help. If the percentage gets too high, however, we must face the accusation of hoarding dollars that could be used more beneficially to spread the gospel now. Decide on a reasonable and realistic percentage, one that will leave you enough to live modestly without anxiety, then lay that amount aside faithfully.

Establishing this figure at a moderate level will keep you from becoming a slave to your bank account, too. Some folks are so afraid of what the future may hold that they become miserly, pinching every penny and making themselves and everyone around them miserable. Like the people who need one more thing to be happy, these people need a little more money in the bank to feel secure. Life has passed them by before they realize that they never really enjoyed living or the good things God has given them.

After giving our government and our God their part, then laying aside a small sum for savings, the final principle for managing our money is to live within the rest of our income. We must make sure that our regular living expenses do not exceed the amount we have left. The exhortation to owe no man anything would obviously require this.[21] If you feel that the Lord would permit you to buy on time, make sure the payments can be made without exceeding the amount you have to work with. Refuse to let yourself buy anything that will cause your expenses to exceed the funds available. A budget will be helpful, but do not be so tied to your budget that you become upset whenever it must be adjusted slightly. Buying at sales will help you stretch your money. Planning menus and buying only the food you need can save you dollars at the grocery store. While you are there, remember that some brands are less expensive than others. You need not buy the best. There are many books available to help you get more for your dollar. Take time to read some of them as part of your Christian stewardship.

It would also be advisable to keep accurate records, so that you

[21]Romans 13:8.

will know where your money has gone. Whether the husband or the wife actually writes the checks is not nearly so important as agreeing on what the money is to be spent for and knowing where it has gone. The only exception to this rule is a small amount which both husband and the wife should enjoy free of mutual accounting. Sometimes husbands feel free to spend money on personal pleasures but deny their wives the same privilege. Be fair with each other.

If you follow these simple principles of finance, your bills will be paid, your testimony will be protected, your marriage will be enhanced, and your Savior will be honored!

# CHAPTER THIRTEEN

# HOW FAIR IS THY LOVE!

Much to the surprise of some Christians, sex was God's idea! "Male and female created he them . . . And God saw everything that he had made, and behold, it was very good . . . Therefore shall a man leave his father and mother, and shall cleave unto his wife; and they shall be one flesh."[1] God created men and women with physical differences that complement each other, and he pronounced it good. He indicated that a husband and a wife should adhere to each other and become "one flesh," a reference primarily to their sexual union.[2] Sex is part of God's plan for the human race.

God made the sexual union of husband and wife to be both pure and pleasurable; both sacred and satisfying. The writer to the Hebrews reveals its sanctity by declaring the marriage bed to be undefiled.[3] Other passages, such as the one in Proverbs, indicate its sheer joy: "Let your manhood be a blessing; rejoice in the wife of your youth. Let her charms and tender embrace satisfy you. Let her love alone fill you with delight."[4] While some wonderful spiritual applications can be made from the Song of Solomon, it can hardly be denied that the Book refers to the sexual experiences of a husband and wife. In utter delight and appreciation, the bridegroom affectionately exclaims to his bride, "How fair is thy love!"[5]

Unfortunately, the sex life of many Christian couples is anything but beautiful. It is instead the source of deep dissatisfaction and repeated disagreements. During their courtship days the couple eagerly anticipated marriage, thinking it would relieve their sexual frustrations and result in instant paradise. The honeymoon shattered the illusion. The first week's crises were followed by many more as the years passed. Finally they concluded that good sexual adjust-

---

[1]Genesis 1:27, 31; 2:24, KJV.   [2]1 Corinthians 6:16.   [3]Hebrews 13:4.
[4]Proverbs 5:18, 19, TLB.   [5]Song of Solomon 4:10, KJV.

ment does not come naturally — that it takes time and effort and a great deal of unselfishness.

So widespread are the problems of sexual adjustment in marriage that many family counselors rank it as a principal cause for marital discord. God says sex is good. Many people say it is a problem in their marriage. Why the difference of opinion? Why do Christian couples have such problems in their sex relationship?

One pitfall is the practice of sex before or outside marriage. Almost all good things can be misused. Food is good, but too much of it or the wrong kind can bring discomfort or disease. Fire is useful, but when it is misused it brings destruction and death. God says that sex within the bonds of marriage is beautiful and blessed, but outside these limits it is dirty, ugly, and sinful. Premarital or extramarital sexual experiences can be a mammoth hindrance to a satisfactory sex life in marriage.

We live in a day of growing permissiveness. While animal-like promiscuity is universally rejected by almost all professing Christians, premarital permissiveness is becoming increasingly tolerated. The idea seems to be that if two people truly love each other, there is no reason why they should not enjoy the full expression of their love right now. The only satisfactory answer I can find lies in the couple's personal relationship with their Lord. If they think anything of him at all, they will certainly want to listen to what he says, and he has said a great deal about this subject in both the Old and New Testaments.

The Apostle Paul writes, "For this is the will of God, even your sanctification, that ye abstain from fornication."[6] The word "fornication" refers to all sexual intercourse outside the bonds of marriage, whether premarital or extramarital. No matter how deeply a man and a woman may feel for each other, God says that it is

[6] 1 Thessalonians 4:3, KJV.

his will for them to abstain from illicit sexual intercourse. If he commands them to abstain, he will give them the grace to obey.

The Apostle goes on to amplify this concept: "That no man go beyond and defraud his brother in the matter."[7] Fornication defrauds other people; it robs them of their rightful affections. It also robs them of their virginity, which should be presented to their future spouse. It likewise robs them of their self-respect — the precious possession of a clear conscience. Even if the thought of robbery does not prevent you from indulging, read on: ". . . because the Lord is the avenger of all such." He can avenge your self-willed disobedience in various ways — veneral disease, unwanted pregnancy, guilt feelings, or lurking suspicion. Some will say, "But medical science and progressive attitudes are eliminating these dangers." None of these prevent God from rendering just vengeance; he is greater than antibiotics, contraceptives, or current community attitudes. If you are now dating, God wants you to map out a carefully planned strategy that will allow you to enjoy each other's company and get to know each other well without indulging in sexually stimulating activities.

Maybe some are saying, "We're married now, but the scars of past guilt and the seeds of past suspicion are sabotaging our sex lives. What can we do?" Each party can acknowledge the wrong he has committed against the other, asking forgiveness for his own part of the blame. Each can confess his sin to God. He is a merciful Father, ready to forgive. The sweet assurance of forgiveness from both your mate and your Lord will help you make a new beginning in this most important area of your life.

A second obstacle to a satisfying sex life seems to be improper attitudes toward sex. Some Christians think sex is dirty and sinful, a necessary act for the perpetuation of the race but certainly not a legitimate enjoyment. They hesitate to mention the subject and be-

[7] 1 Thessalonians 4:6, KJV.

come embarrassed by reading even sanctified literature on the subject. They forget that the greatest Book of all, the Word of God, has much to say about sex! If God thinks sex is important enough to discuss, we ought to examine what he says. Paul, inspired by the Holy Spirit, advised the Christians at Corinth about sex, and God saw fit to preserve it in his Word. He knew that we would probably need the same advice.

"Nevertheless, to avoid fornication, let every man have his own wife, and let every woman have her own husband."[8] The purpose of sex is not merely for procreation, but to satisfy a biological need that we would be tempted to satisfy sinfully were it not for marriage. Paul recognizes that this drive is present in both men and women. A woman should have a husband in order to help her avoid fornication, just as a man should have a wife to help him avoid fornication. Even though some people have thought otherwise, it is normal and wholesome for a wife to have sexual desires, just as it is for her husband. While a woman's desires are usually less intense than a man's, it is interesting to note that God has placed an organ in the female body, the clitoris, which serves no function except to provide a pleasurable sensation. He must have wanted her to enjoy physical relations with her husband!

One purpose for sex, then, is to satisfy a legitimate physical desire. This appetite must sometimes be subjugated or sublimated, with physical energies redirected and released in other ways, as in the case of an unmarried person or a sickly spouse. Unlike the requirement for food, sexual needs can be sublimated by properly chosen substitute activities. By God's grace single people can live a well-balanced life without indulging in sin. However, God's normal plan is for couples to marry and to fully satisfy each others sexual needs.

The passage goes on to state, "The man should give his wife all that is her right as a married woman, and the wife should do the

[8] 1 Corinthians 7:2, KJV.

same for her husband."[9] Here we are clearly told that a husband and a wife are responsible to meet each other's sexual needs. But this is far more than a burdensome obligation; for a man and a woman deeply in love with each other it is a joyous and delightful privilege. God has constructed their bodies is such a way that the mutual fulfilling of sexual needs becomes the ultimate expression of self-giving love, bringing exquisite enjoyment to both husband and wife.

Sex as God planned it is not simply the expression of an urge or the satisfaction of a need. It is the giving of our bodies to express the deepest feelings of love that lie within us, and it results in the rapturous enjoyment of the one we love. God says that my body belongs to my wife for her gratification and pleasure, and that her body belongs to me for my satisfaction and delight. While modesty is the rule in public, the total enjoyment of each other's bodies is a wholesome, God-ordained privilege behind closed bedroom doors.

Paul teaches in First Corinthians 7:3 and 4 that husbands and wives share equal privileges in the ownership of each other's bodies. It is not sinful for a husband to desire his wife's body. A Spirit-filled husband in love with his wife will admire, fondle, kiss, and caress his wife's body as an expression of his love for her, thereby meeting her needs as well as his own. A Spirit-filled wife in love with her husband will thrill him immensely by letting him know she desires his body and enjoys meeting his needs. Even a casual reading of the Song of Solomon will show that the wife's body delighted her husband[10] and the husband's body brought pleasure to his wife.[11] Nowhere does the Bible limit the variety of ways in which a husband and wife may bring physical pleasure to each other through their bodies, assuming that each finds it mutually pleasurable and neither finds it objectionable. The only limitation is love, which will cause us to place the feelings of our mates above our own desires.

---

[9] 1 Corinthians 7:3, TLB.    [10] Song of Solomon 4:1-7; 6:4-9; 7:1-9.    [11] Song of Solomon 5:10-16.

There is still another thought in Paul's advice to the Corinthians regarding sex. "Defraud ye not one the other, except it be with consent for a time, that ye may give yourselves to fasting and prayer; and come together again, that Satan tempt you not for your incontinency."[12] Some Christians seem to have the notion that it is highly spiritual to abstain from sexual intercourse, that Spirit-filled believers are just not very interested in this kind of thing. Sometimes wives will deny their husbands sexual rights because of their own unbiblical attitudes toward sex, or as an attempt to retaliate for some injustice, or possibly even because they consider themselves too spiritual. But God regards this as theft — the deprivation of a legitimate enjoyment. Instead of being spiritual, the refusal to provide intercourse is disobedience to God.

There will probably be abstinence during the wife's menstrual period. There will be periods of time when, by mutual consent, a couple will abstain in order to give themselves uninterruptedly to prayer over some pressing issue. There may be times when one simply does not feel like having relations. The other will not force the matter but will in unselfish love graciously refrain for the good of the one loved. But they will soon resume their normal relations with whatever frequency they have found to be mutually satisfying, lest Satan tempt them to an illicit affair.

We have mentioned Spirit-filled believers. Rather than hindering a satisfying sex life, the filling of the Spirit will enhance it. When the Lord Jesus Christ is in complete control of our lives we will be supremely unselfish, and unselfishness is the key to a successful sex life. Unselfishness causes one to recognize the inherent differences between men and women sexually, then to treat one's mate accordingly. For example, it is common knowledge that the sight of a woman's body can bring a man to readiness for sexual relations.

---

[12] 1 Corinthians 7:5, KJV.

Women, on the other hand, generally respond much more slowly, and to long and tender caresses. A wife will not be disturbed at her husband for his more frequent advances, nor will a husband be upset with his wife for her apparent disinterest. She will try to respond to him graciously; he will patiently take the time to meet her needs. Both will realize that there will be some occasions when her only desire is to bring him satisfaction.

Letting the Holy Spirit control our lives will help in other ways as well. The most successful sexual experiences grow out of warm and precious fellowship enjoyed hours and days before sexual union. The Holy Spirit is the One who can help us develop this warm and loving personal intimacy. The self-giving love which he produces in the lives of both husband and wife will draw them to each other sexually, so that they can experience ultimate expression and complete fulfillment of their love. He gives us the desire to interact with each other graciously all through the day, rather than regarding each other merely as playthings to be enjoyed selfishly at bedtime. Sex that grows naturally out of this kind of warm and loving relationship is sex at its best. Spirit-inspired love can adequately meet and successfully solve almost any problem in a couple's sex life.

This chapter was obviously not intended to provide a detailed description of sexual techniques. It was simply intended to help establish proper attitudes toward sex by examining what God has to say about the subject. These proper attitudes are necessary before we can even begin to use any sex techniques successfully.

If we have learned anything at all from the Scriptures, it has been that sex in marriage is not shameful, but holy. The Bible deals with it frankly and openly, and so should we. The best way to resolve problems in this area is to keep the lines of communication open. Husbands and wives need to tell each other kindly but candidly what they enjoy, what brings them greatest pleasure, and how they feel their sex lives can be improved. Discussing the subject calmly and prayerfully with each other will melt down the obstacles and make sex the beautiful experience God intended it to be.